RESPONSE TO MUSIC

RESPONSE TO MUSIC

PRINCIPLES OF MUSIC EDUCATION

by

BRIAN BROCKLEHURST
M.A., D.Mus.

Routledge & Kegan Paul

LONDON

First published in 1971 by
Routledge & Kegan Paul Limited
Broadway House, 68–74 Carter Lane,
London E.C.4V. 5E.L.
Printed in Great Britain by
Alden & Mowbray Ltd
at the Alden Press, Oxford
© Brian Brocklehurst 1971

ISBN 0 7100 6949 9

CONTENTS

FOREWORD

This book is concerned with the role of music in education, the formulation of aims and objectives and the relationship between values, aims and teaching methods.

Since they must be dynamic and related to changing social needs, aims cannot have universal applicability. The relationship of aims in music education to the requirements of our modern technological society is examined and attention given to the adaptability of various foreign systems of music education.

Particular reference is made to those aims concerned with the development of musical responsiveness: some of the principal factors determining responsiveness are considered and their educational implications discussed. To two of these factors, musical understanding and skills, separate chapters are devoted.

BRIAN BROCKLEHURST

The University of Birmingham

FOREWORD

EDUCATIVE VALUES

THE ROLE OF MUSIC IN EDUCATION

In spite of the remarkable advances made in the field of musical education in recent years, music continues to be in many ways one of the Cinderella subjects of the school curriculum. According to the Newsom Report[1] 'music is frequently the worst equipped and accommodated subject in the curriculum', less than a quarter of the schools having specially designed music rooms and half having none. Moreover, time-table provision gives the unfortunate impression that music becomes less important as children get older: over one-third of the boys' schools referred to in the Newsom Report and seven per cent of the co-educational schools have no music in the fourth year. Time-table provision in many boys' grammar schools is also quite inadequate. The wide variation in the provision made for music by local education authorities and the failure of some of them to appoint music advisers is further evidence of the lack of true recognition of music's educative value.

This unsatisfactory state of affairs may be due in part

to the fact that many of the arguments advanced in favour of music in education have been insufficiently persuasive and that inadequate attention has been given to the formulation of realistic aims and objectives. A number of widely-held misconceptions regarding the nature of music and musicality have proved a further complication. The argument that extra-curricular musical activities are of greater value than formal class lessons fails to take account of the need to make adequate musical provision for those children lacking in executive ability and the importance of providing a progressive and systematic course in music.

The fact that music is not an easily examinable subject has been partly responsible for its exclusion from the group of prestige subjects. Unattractive and unenterprising syllabuses and the problems involved in making adequate time-table provision have resulted in a small number of candidates taking music in the G.C.E. examination. The number taking 'O' level music is 13·5% of that taking art and thus ranks with book-keeping, metalwork, economics and Spanish. Approximately 1·5% of the total of 'A' level candidates offer music, geology and Spanish, compared with 8·3% offering art. It is to be hoped that recently-introduced improvements in certain G.C.E. syllabuses will lead to some increase in the proportion of candidates taking music and that the interest aroused by C.S.E. syllabuses will contribute to an improvement in music's educational image.

It is possible to see in the lack of recognition accorded to music in education a reflection of society's attitude to the arts in general. They tend to be regarded as an attractive adornment and embellishment rather than a vital educational force and an integral part of the curriculum.

It is thus important for a closer study to be made of

the role of music in education. Just as educational aims determine content and method, so aims are determined by beliefs in educative values. It is clearly essential for the teacher of music to be convinced that music is an indispensable constituent of a truly liberal education. Such a conviction will determine the enthusiasm, vitality and quality of his teaching and prevent his being unduly discouraged by inadequate time-table, accommodation and equipment provision or overwhelmed and exhausted by a wide range of extra-curricular musical activities. The same genuine sense of conviction will be important if he is called upon to justify the considerable expense involved in a comprehensive programme of musical education. But not only must he be able to convince colleagues and education officials; his pupils are likely to question increasingly the purpose and value of what they are expected to study. An awareness on the part of pupils of the purposes of and benefits to be derived from the study of a subject can profoundly influence their attitude towards the subject and, consequently, the quality of their learning.

The changes in educationists' views about the value of music have to some extent reflected changes in social values and political and social theories. Aristotle regarded music as an essential factor in education because of its great influence in character-building. Medieval monastery and cathedral schools were primarily vocational establishments in that their principal function was to provide musical training for boys and youths engaged in the singing of the church services. In the medieval universities,[2] music was a valued subject of the Quadrivium because it was believed that it trained the mind in abstract speculation; students received instruction in plainsong and the teachings of Boethius, incorporated in *De institutione Musica* and revised in the eleventh century by Johannes de Muris. Music's subsequent decline in educational importance can be attributed in part to the dissolution of the monasteries and chantries, the division between grammar and song schools, which at first had been so closely associated, and to the increasing secularization of education. For Milton,[3] the purpose of music in education was merely to provide a means of relaxation and recreation for students between more important activities. John Locke deplored the amount of time young men devoted to learning to play musical instruments, while Miss Bingley, in *Pride and Prejudice*, included 'a thorough knowledge of music' in her list of requirements for an 'accomplished' woman. In nineteenth-century state schools music was regarded as an important moralizing force. Specially composed songs of a crudely didactic nature were intended to inculcate habits of industry and truthfulness and it was believed that the 'refining influence' of such words as in the following verse would help to soften children's 'turbulent spirits':

> Be kind to thy father—for now he is old,
> His locks intermingled with grey,
> His footsteps are feeble, once fearless and bold,
> Thy father is passing away.

Fortunately the folk song revival in the 1890s resulted in children being provided with more valuable vocal fare.

The twentieth century has seen a return to the Renaissance conception of the education of the whole man; as the Newsom Report observes, 'the value of the educational experience should be assessed in terms of its total impact on the pupils' skill, qualities and personal development, not by basic attainments alone'.

EMOTIONAL DEVELOPMENT

The most obvious aspect of music's functional role in

education is that concerned with emotional development. Reference is frequently made to the need for education to be concerned with developing qualities of both heart and intellect and to the importance of healthy emotional development, especially of the environmentally and culturally deprived, to counteract the coarsening and dehumanizing influences of our increasingly materialistic society. Throughout history, music has probably been the most pervasive of the arts, having entered the most fully into the lives of individuals and communities. The quality of life would be immeasurably poorer without music; Kodály declared it to be as much a necessity as air and Ruskin ranked it with food, shelter and raiment as one of the four necessities of life.

Many attempts have been made to explain the unique satisfaction that people of all societies derive from music. It has been suggested that aesthetic experience, which can clarify and enrich emotional life, is a fundamental human need because man is essentially a symbol-producing organism.[4] This algedonic theory of aesthetics is based on the assumption that through art, man is able to symbolize his experience. Life, like art, is characterized by a constant flux and adjustment to environment: disequilibrium–equilibrium, ebb–flow, tension–release, stimulus–repose, need–fulfilment. Thus from any natural or artistic phenomena, such as discord-resolution in music, which reflect the stress–release pattern of man's ordinary experience, he derives aesthetic pleasure.

Psycho-physiological studies which have been made of the effects of music on posture, respiration, galvanic skin response and vascular change emphasize the close interaction between physical and mental processes and explain the initial emotional reaction to music on the nervous system.[5] These studies provide impressive evidence of the deep penetrability of music and of the directness and immediacy of its emotional appeal.

A further reason for the value of music as a source of emotional enrichment and refreshment is that it is a unique form of non-verbal communication. According to the Crowther Report,[6] education is 'so highly and necessarily verbalised . . . that it needs a counterpoise'. Moreover verbal communication is inevitably restricted by the degree of identity of experience between the parties involved. Music can thus be a valuable substitute for verbal communication, particularly for those who are linguistically or emotionally handicapped. Communication is a two-way process, involving the concept of interchange, and inability to communicate results in anxiety, frustration and a sense of inadequacy which, in turn, can produce either aggressive, anti-social behaviour, or a withdrawn state of helplessness. The most extreme form of the latter state occurs in the case of the autistic psychotic; such a child may perhaps be reached through music because of its non-verbal character, its deep penetrability and the fact that it is so difficult to erect a defence mechanism against its effects. Music may be similarly valuable in cases of aphasia, where the speech area of the brain is undeveloped or damaged.

Because of its non-verbal nature, music is an emotionally flexible and ambiguous art form. The music of Mozart, with its infinity of meanings, recalls Keats's reference to joy and melancholy being inseparably linked because of their 'fugitive nature':

> . . . in the very temple of delight
> Veil'd Melancholy has her sovran shrine.

Music's ambiguity is one of the secrets of its power, for we are able to draw from it according to our intellectual

6

and emotional needs. Not only can less able or mal-adjusted children project their emotional conflicts into the music they hear; they can discover in music an important means of creative self-expression. The inarticulate are incapable of, and the withdrawn wary of, verbal precision in communicating their feelings, whereas they are likely to be more able and willing to express themselves through music.

The qualities of music discussed so far have led to its use for a wide variety of purposes. In the cinema and theatre music's remarkable evocative power may be used to create an appropriate atmosphere or intensify the emotional impact of a scene. The effects of music are also increasingly exploited by commercial interests. Music's wide emotional range, its directness of impact and communicative qualities have led, in recent years, to an increasingly close study of ways in which the controlled use of music and its principal elements can contribute to psychotherapeutic practice and some branches of remedial education.[7]

INTELLECTUAL DEVELOPMENT

Classification of subjects of the curriculum as intellectual or aesthetic is misleading. It would be quite wrong to imply that music and the other arts have a monopoly of aesthetic value in education; mathematics, for instance, has a considerable aesthetic appeal. Similarly, it is not only such subjects as Latin and mathematics which contribute towards intellectual development. Music has frequently been referred to as an activity of the mind: hence the considerable amount of research which has been carried out into the psychology of music. It can provide an intellectual stimulus and satisfaction com-

7

parable to that of any of the more 'academic' subjects. Indeed it was for this reason that it occupied such an honoured place in the medieval Quadrivium. It is true that there is a low correlation between general intelligence, as measured by tests of verbal reasoning, and musical ability, as measured by tests of sensory capacity. However, real achievement in the highly-skilled craft of music demands a number of abilities, such as the ability to create pattern and perceive relationships, which are in fact functions of general intelligence; listening skills, too, involve judgment and tonal memory and require sustained and concentrated attention. Music has a language and literature of its own and an advanced study of its history and linguistic features can be an exacting discipline, making strenuous intellectual demands. The senses have been described as 'the gateways of knowledge' and it is certainly true that sensory training plays a vital part in intellectual development. Music not only makes a valuable contribution to the development of auditory perception, which has been neglected in other subjects. It can also involve visual, tactile and kinaesthetic imagery, particularly in music and movement, music reading and instrumental playing. This may partially explain the superior general educational achievements claimed for children in Hungarian music primary schools to those of children in Hungary's other primary schools, in spite of the greater amount of time devoted in the latter to 'academic' subjects.[8]

PHYSICAL DEVELOPMENT

Motor imagery plays an important part in music. In this sense, music is an activity subject which can contribute towards physical development in a variety of ways. Thus music and movement can benefit the physically-awkward, a-rhythmic child by relaxing muscular tension, developing co-ordination of mind and body and by providing an outlet for emotional tension and an opportunity for creative self-expression. Singing and the playing of wind instruments can assist respiratory development because of the emphasis they place upon correct posture, lung capacity and diaphragmatic control. These activities can also help in cases of defective speech; woodwind playing develops the musculature in the lips and cheeks and brass playing involves rhythmic articulation of the tongue. Rudolf Steiner, the founder of Anthroposophy, maintained that, since music is an expression of cosmic surge and flow, divine healing forces can enter into us through music. He believed that there is a close association between musical rhythm and the body's circulatory and respiratory system, between melody and the nervous system and harmony and the metabolic system.[9] Although one may be inclined to dismiss the claims made by some of Steiner's disciples for the value of music in the treatment of heart disease, tuberculosis and cancer, there is ample evidence to suggest that music, particularly in the form of instrumental playing, can make an important contribution to the education of the physically handicapped. Both the Wingfield Club and Valence School orchestras provide a means of physical and social rehabilitation in addition to the opportunity to develop a potential leisure-time pursuit. Much research has been carried out into ways of adapting instruments and ingenious devices and supports have been made to enable instruments to be played with deformed hands or with only one hand. Others working in this field have argued that, since physical handicaps are frequently accompanied by emotional problems, unadapted instruments should be used to encourage, indeed challenge, players to over-come their particular disabilities and thereby to develop confidence through a sense of achievement.

Music can also be an important element in the educa-tion of children with sensory handicaps, especially the visually handicapped. Although there is no evidence to suggest that blind children have greater innate musical ability than others, they do possess more highly developed auditory perception as well as interest in and memory for sound. Because music will be a leisure-time interest for most of them and a means of livelihood for some, it is essential that blind children be provided with as compre-hensive and systematic a course in music as possible. Singing can assist the development of the speaking voice, which is so important a means of communication for the blind, and instrumental playing and movement can be interesting forms of sensory-motor training. Although the learning of Braille musical notation constitutes a serious problem, blind children can make great progress in the acquisition of creative and listening skills.

Even in the education of the deaf, music has a contribu-tion to make. Technical developments in means of amplifying sounds and refinements in hearing aids are enabling teachers of deaf children to exploit more fully their remnants of hearing. Music can be used in such children's exploration of varied forms of communication, for their more highly developed sense of touch and vibration enables them to receive sound through the vibratory channels. Thus sound can be received as vibration through the hands and feet or, in the case of clarinet playing, through the upper teeth. The child who is deprived of sound is deprived also of rhythm. Hence the value in his education of music and movement, singing and percussion playing, for these activities can assist the process of acquiring language by developing rhythmic speech and correct verbal accentuation. It is possible to awaken and develop rudimentary pitch sense as well as rhythmic sense. Frequency range is as important as dynamic level, for notes of different pitches can be felt in different parts of the body. The question of suitable register is one of the factors influencing the choice of music to be played, perhaps via multiple hearing aids connected to a record player.

SOCIAL DEVELOPMENT

Music can appeal to both the most withdrawn and the most gregarious of children, for it is at once one of the most intimate and most socialized art forms. Since it provides so many varied opportunities for shared experience and collective participation, music can develop social awareness and integration and thus play a significant part in the process of social maturation. Recently-developed group music-making activities, catering for a wide range of abilities and interests, can cut across intellectual and social barriers. Children who are in need of social rehabilitation and adjustment to their environment can feel that they are sharing in and contributing to a joint venture, without losing their individual identity; their awareness of the fact that, since they have something to offer, they are an asset rather than a liability to their group can have an important integrating effect. Opportunities to make music for, as well as with, others can also contribute to developing a sense of social significance and utility. Group activities in music enable children to exercise individual initiative and responsibility and to learn various important qualities of behaviour associated with social competence and the development of satisfactory human relationships: co-operation, consideration, responsibility, self-control and self-discipline are essential in ensemble work and, through such activities, children learn to differentiate between team spirit and mere herd instinct.

Activities involving singing, instrumental playing and movement, organized on a class basis, enable each child to contribute at his own level. Listening also involves a shared experience: there is a significant psychological difference between solitary and shared listening because of the influence of 'passive sympathy' on the latter response.

Other differently-constituted groups, of varying sizes, can also have socially-integrating values. Such groups form psychological units since their members are welded together by common interests, skills and objectives. In this sense, group instrumental tuition may have certain advantages over individual tuition. It is true that, since group instruction can make only limited provision for differences in aptitude, groups for beginners should not be too large and should become progressively smaller as the pupils advance. However, much depends on the skill of the teacher in recognizing the importance of shared experience in developing interest and confidence. The skilful teacher will therefore ensure that opportunities are provided in the early stages for ensemble experience. The violin class movement dates back to the nineteenth century; the piano class movement has a similarly long history but has never met with the same success, although in the United States in recent years there has developed an increasing interest in the use of electronic piano laboratories. The popularity of recorder playing in so many schools, the availability of less expensive instruments made possible by the introduction of new materials and methods of mass production, the fact that it is possible to make more obvious progress in the initial stages of learning wind instruments and their possibly greater appeal to many boys are some of the reasons for the growth of the wind-class movement in schools. This growth may be responsible for the fact that the piano accounted for only 79% of the practical entries for Associated Board examinations in 1965, compared with 94% in 1946.

The increasing emphasis on group instrumental tuition has led to a considerable widening in the scope of orchestral and ensemble playing in schools. The brass band movement continues to flourish and interest in the advantages of symphonic wind bands is likely to develop, for such bands can provide ensemble opportunities for the increasing number of wind players in schools who cannot be absorbed into conventional orchestras.

Choirs are also obvious socializing influences since they can play such an important part in the social and ceremonial life of schools. They can secure continuity of experience in cases where class music is not organized throughout the school; they provide the opportunity to perform extended works which would be beyond the technical capacity of the ordinary singing class and thus prepare for interest in adult choral singing. The opportunity to exercise leadership, which is so important in social education, may be provided by encouraging older pupils to get together and direct smaller choirs; such choirs, together with other instrumental and vocal ensembles, may take part in inter-house competitions, organized on the lines of an Eisteddfod. The scope of school music can be extended to include stage and concert performances of nativity, ballad, and chamber operas: the opera provides a splendid opportunity for correlation since it is a project involving a widely-varied range of activities.

Music can exert a unifying, vitalizing influence on the life and 'tone' of a school and help to develop a corporate spirit: hence the important part played by music in such school functions and formal occasions as morning assembly, speech days and carol concerts. Choral, orchestral and operatic activities can provide opportunities for pupil–teacher–parent collaboration and thus contribute to the development of a sense of community.

Although it is desirable to achieve a unified social pattern and enable children to realize the essential oneness of a school as a community, schools should not be isolated social organisms. The varied musical activities in Harlow New Town, for instance, have shown how music can enrich the quality of community life in a newly-developed area. Through music, schools can develop useful contacts with neighbouring schools. Nearby boys' and girls' schools can form joint orchestras, choirs and music societies and members of school orchestras can combine to form local youth orchestras: in 1965 the National Association of Youth Orchestras was established to co-ordinate the work of such orchestras throughout the country. Several local authorities have formed junior music schools to provide tuition in piano-playing and general musicianship as well as the playing of orchestral instruments; these Saturday morning schools are particularly valuable to promising instrumentalists coming from smaller schools. With the establishment of music centres in a number of areas, the scope of work of the junior music schools has been considerably broadened.

Different types of music festival have also enabled neighbouring schools to work together. The non-competitive festival movement came into existence

largely as a result of the work of Ulric Brunner, a Shrop-
shire headmaster, and in 1927 the first such festival was
held at Bridgnorth. A non-competitive festival generally
begins with the director listening to the performances
given by the various schools. Teachers are given the
director's written comments and also have the opportunity to meet the director informally for further discussion. This may be followed by a rehearsal of combined
choirs in preparation for a concert. The Farnham and
Leicestershire festivals are also organized on a regional
basis. The first Farnham Festival was held in 1963 and
over one thousand children from twenty schools have
performed works specially commissioned by local busi-
ness concerns; the first Leicestershire Festival was held
in 1965.

A notable advance in school orchestral work in recent
years has been the great increase in the number of summer
schools and residential courses for young instrumentalists
and the formation of several youth orchestras and bands,
organized on a national basis. These include the National
Youth Orchestra of Great Britain, formed in 1947, the
British Youth Symphony Orchestra, formed in 1956 by
the Schools Music Association, and the National Youth
Brass Band of Great Britain, formed in 1952. One of the
few choral organizations for youth is 'Sing for Pleasure',
formed in 1964. This is the English branch of the 'A
Cœur Joie' choral movement, founded by César Geoffray.
It is intended for the 16 to 25 age group and holds three
weekend meetings each year.

Several local and national youth orchestras have performed abroad and some have made exchange visits with
foreign youth orchestras. Music, being an international
language and tool of communication, can transcend
national boundaries. One of the reasons for the founding

in 1947 of the International Folk Music Council was that folk song and dance could be a medium for understanding and form a bond between people of different nations. The study of folk music, by providing insight into the cultural patterns of different racial groups, can assist the process of integration in our increasingly multi-racial society and make some contribution to the development of international understanding and a sense of world citizenship.

Some of the ways have been discussed in which music can contribute to the emotional, intellectual, physical and social development of children. These various aspects of development are of course closely inter-related. Thus intellectual or social growth is likely to be hindered by emotional difficulties. A physical handicap or intellectual or emotional retardation is also likely to have a deleterious effect on social development and a feeling of isolation and exclusion, which may be produced by differences in ability, speech, physique, dress or taste, can have an inhibiting effect on both personal and social growth; hence the significance of the term 'social individuality', which implies a single conception of self-realization and social competence.

INTRINSIC AND EXTRINSIC VALUES

It may be argued that, in discussing the role of music in education, too much emphasis should not be placed on instrumental, functional values for they are subsidiary, ancillary, non-musical and extrinsic. It has also been somewhat cynically observed that a surprisingly large number of professional musicians succeed in developing a remarkable immunity to music's many allegedly beneficial effects. It is certainly true that music should not be regarded as a mere accessory to education and that only in some branches of remedial education may music be legitimately regarded as a means to non-musical ends. Moreover, as the Norwood Report[10] pointed out, there is a danger in attempting to justify and recommend subjects 'with pleas which may at some time diminish in cogency as educational or psychological theory changes'; thus certain values claimed for music in the past cannot be substantiated because they derive from out-moded faculty psychology. Those who would rely exclusively on music's intrinsic values maintain that it is possible to find in music what cannot be found elsewhere, that music plays a unique role and thus needs no external justification. Excessive emphasis on unique, special and distinctive values, however, can widen still further the harmful gap between music and the other subjects of the curriculum. There is really no sharp dividing line between intrinsic and extrinsic values, between education in music and education through music: the development of musical responsiveness is both a means and an end.

NOTES TO CHAPTER I

1 Newsom Report, *Half our Future*, H.M.S.O., 1963.

2 Carpenter, N. C., *Music in the Medieval and Renaissance Universities*, University of Oklahoma Press, 1958.

3 Milton, J., *Of Education: Letter to Master Samuel Hartlib*, 1644.

4 Langer, S. K., *Feeling and Form*, New York: Charles Scribner's Sons, 1953.

5 Henkin, R. J., 'The Prediction of Behaviour Response Patterns to Music', *Journal of Psychology*, xliv (1957).

6 Crowther Report, *15 to 18*, H.M.S.O., 1959.

7 Alvin, J., *Music Therapy*, John Baker, 1966.

8 Sándor, F. (ed.), *Musical Education in Hungary*, Barrie & Rockliff, 1966.

9 Stebbing, L. (ed.), *Music and Healing*, New Knowledge Books, 1963.

10 Norwood Report, *Curriculum and Examinations in Secondary Schools*, H.M.S.O., 1941.

AIMS

THE IMPORTANCE OF AIMS

It is essential to apply rigorous and critical thought to the role of music in education if realistic and clearly delineated aims and objectives are to be formulated and if unity, cohesion and coherence are to be achieved in the curriculum. A teacher's aims are determined by his views on the educative values of his subject and, in turn, determine the content of his lessons, his choice of materials and methods of presentation, for the latter are simply means through which goals can be realized and objectives attained. It is clear then that values, aims and methods are closely inter-related and that the more sharply-defined are a teacher's aims, the more effective is his teaching likely to be. Well-formulated aims, based on a genuine conviction about educative values, can vitalize a teacher's work, give it a sense of purpose and direction and thereby help to counteract the discouraging factors referred to in the last chapter. Pupils also need to have their own goals and thus must be aware of the underlying aims of their curricular experiences and understand their function and relevance. One of the results of learner-centred education is that older pupils no longer regard themselves as uncritical receiver organisms and therefore, as mentioned in the previous chapter, they increasingly question the purpose and relevance of what they are expected to learn. Lack of understanding about objectives and dissatisfaction with teaching methods have been contributory causes of the upheaval in universities and colleges in so many parts of the world and may lead to unrest in schools also.

British teachers enjoy a much greater degree of freedom in choice of content and method than, for example, do French teachers. The latter are required to teach according to syllabuses prepared by the central authorities. In music, for instance, detailed schemes of work are drawn up for vocal, aural and rhythm training, singing, solfège and musical history. School music in France, unlike that in Britain, is thus lacking in any tradition of individual initiative, experimentation, flexibility, diversity or variety of pattern. Although central control can have a beneficial effect on continuity and reduce the likelihood of disparity in musical provision between schools, it is generally agreed that school music in France compares very unfavourably with that in Britain. The freedom of British teachers is, of course, not absolute: external examination requirements, the need to be aware of music's relationship to the total curriculum of a school and the views of headteachers, governors, inspectors, advisers, colleagues and parents are, to some extent, restricting influences. Nonetheless, the degree of freedom is such that it places considerable responsibility on teachers to formulate their own educational goals and to translate these into terms of content and method.

Educational aims are also important because they form

the basis of evaluation. The effectiveness of teaching methods and materials and the quality of learning can be assessed only in relation to carefully thought out long-term and specific short-term goals. Frequent and regular evaluation of individual lessons as well as of courses is also important if we are to judge the validity of the aims and objectives we set. Considerable attention has been given in the United States to the devising of evaluative methods and techniques and different types of standardized test have been used as evaluative instruments and measuring devices. Thus, in addition to prognostic tests of musical ability, there exist diagnostic tests of achievement, notation tests and measures of instrumental and sight-singing skills, musical appreciation and taste.[1] Unfortunately the more important aspects of musical education are extremely difficult to measure and therefore these various evaluative devices, including those allegedly concerned with appreciation and taste, are restricted in scope, concentrate on areas of knowledge rather than of understanding and provide little indication of children's developing responsiveness to music. Tests of attitudinal patterns of musical behaviour would perhaps be more useful for evaluative purposes. Changes in attitude to music may be measured formally by means of opinion scale techniques and subject preference rankings or informally by noting modifications in musical behaviour, habits, opinions and interests. Borrowing or buying records and books on music, attendance at concerts, membership of choirs, orchestras, instrumental classes, music societies and similar voluntary activities, listening to music on radio and television and the initiative, interest and enthusiasm shown during class music lessons are some of the more obvious ways in which musical attitude is revealed. Some of this information can be noted on

individual record cards, which can also be used for purposes of cumulative measurement and assessment.

It is suggested, then, that clear, realistic aims are of
crucial importance because they determine the method
and quality of teaching, because of the weighty responsibility which must inevitably accompany educational
freedom and the fact that aims are essential for purposes
of evaluation. Ill-conceived aims, lacking in precision
and definition, or the total absence of aims, inevitably
result in ill-focused teaching. Such teaching, especially of
so intangible a subject as music, is frequently lacking in
balance, continuity or any real sense of direction, pro-
gression and purpose. Aimless teaching, which is
accompanied as often as not by class restlessness and
inattention, is partly responsible for the lack of respect
accorded to music in some schools and for the resulting
restricted time-table provision. In other cases, teachers
are so preoccupied with short-term goals that they
neglect ultimate objectives. This results in a confusion
of means and ends, aims and methods; creativity, participation, involvement, skills, correlation and integration
are not aims but simply means to achieving aims. The
absence of meaningful, long-term aims is revealed also
in an uncritical adoption of teaching methods associated
with an earlier era or in feverish anxiety to leap on to
every new educational bandwagon. The absence of such
aims can also result in teaching what is easiest to teach
(the easiest methods are generally the least satisfactory)
or in a teacher's having recourse to a diluted version of
his own training in music. As Tovey warned, 'the only
thing we professional musicians must guard against is the
danger of confusion between knowledge that is relevant
to the understanding of a work of art, and knowledge
which is relevant only to the discipline of an artist's train-

ing'.[2] It is important also to consider the place of public performances in a school's music programme and ways in which they can contribute to the attainment of objectives. Concerts and their preparation can provide valuable educative musical experiences; public approbation, however, should not be the principal goal, nor should the regular music programme be disrupted by excessive use of class-lesson time for rehearsal purposes. If this is allowed to occur, ends are being sacrificed to means. Class music, though perhaps less glamorous than public concerts, is no less important: successful concerts are an inadequate criterion by which to judge a school's total music programme.

PROBLEMS OF FORMULATING AIMS

No set of educational aims, especially short-term ones, can have universal applicability. One reason for this, in the field of musical education, is the ambiguity of so much musical terminology. Thus such terms as 'musical talent' and 'musicality' are used in different senses by Seashore, Schoen and Lundin.[3] 'Musical appreciation' can refer to musical enjoyment, knowledge or discrimination or any combination of these elements. The term 'musicianship', too, is used in different ways. Even the term 'music' itself implies different types of skill in different examination syllabuses and may refer to executive skills or knowledge of the language or literature of music.

In many ways the problem was less complex in the nineteenth century when lessons were labelled 'singing'. The scope of work in singing and sight reading was, of course, very restricted, but within these narrow confines, teachers had little difficulty in formulating precise aims and devising simple evaluative methods. The payment by results system, which was responsible for this narrow approach to school music, resulted from an unfavourable report made by the Newcastle Commission in 1861 on the state of elementary education. Lowe's Revised Code, introduced in the following year, provided that grants for education should henceforth be capitation grants, one-third for attendance and two-thirds for proficiency in basic subjects. When music became a recognized subject for grant purposes, it was decided that a school's annual grant should be reduced by a shilling per scholar in average attendance if singing were not included in the curriculum; in 1882 a distinction was made between singing by rote, which secured a grant of sixpence per pupil, and singing from notation, which secured a grant of one shilling. Although the Revised Code ended in 1897 school music remained very narrow in scope for a number of years; indeed, according to the 1905 edition of *Suggestions for the Consideration of Teachers*, many children were still being taught only five songs.

The gradual increase in range of musical activities in schools has been accompanied by increasingly complex problems of formulating aims and assessing the effectiveness of teaching. Each teacher must solve such problems for himself, for aims and objectives must always be based on an individual teacher's value judgments and be a direct reflection of his philosophies of general as well as of musical education. His specific short-term goals will, of course, be very much influenced by the type of school in which he is teaching. The cultural and socio-economic background of his pupils, the musical tradition of the school and its locality, the available musical accommodation, facilities and equipment, the musical skills and interests of colleagues and the nature of the total school curriculum are factors which the teacher will take into account when formulating his objectives, devising his methods and selecting his materials.

23

AIMS AND SOCIAL NEEDS

A further reason for the fact that educational aims cannot have universal, permanent applicability is that they must be closely related to the changing characteristics and requirements of particular societies. Aims, like the society they serve, must be dynamic and fluid and curricular developments must keep pace with social change and be correctly oriented to social needs. Unless education mirrors and influences the quality of society and current-ly-held social attitudes and values it will, by serving past needs and being aimed at outmoded goals, be providing an education for an obsolescent society. The educational consequences of changing patterns of social behaviour have profound implications for all teachers of music, for the aims they establish must be related to the role of music in society both today and at the beginning of the twenty-first century. The increasing awareness that music is a form of human behaviour and a social pheno-menon, rather than 'an object in itself without reference to the cultural matrix out of which it is produced', has resulted in a growing number of research investigations into musical anthropology and ethnomusicology. Musical educationists also must make a closer study of the sociology of music.[4]

The rate of expansion of our knowledge of the physical and social world and the consequent accelerating pace of technological and scientific advance are causing society to change at an increasingly rapid rate. The population of this country, which may exceed sixty-five million by the end of the century, will continue to move from rural districts and concentrate in huge urban areas. This will result in patterns of urbanization growing enormously in complexity. Society is likely to become much more heterogeneous and multi-racial. There will probably be an increase in social mobility, class distinctions will become less pronounced and the extension of political, social and economic equality will be accompanied by a continuing trend towards egalitarianism. This may result in part from the fact that, with the increase in affluence made possible by technological advance, more and more adolescent and adult workers will aspire to what were formerly middle-class standards of life, tastes and leisure-time pursuits. Social prognostication can also conjure up a nightmarish vision of a depersonalized broiler-house society; in such a society, music could play a more vital aesthetic role than at any other time in the history of mankind.

The restructuring of our educational system, which involves placing the emphasis on providing broad educational opportunities for all and avoiding wastage of potential ability, rather than on selection, pruning and elimination, is likely greatly to benefit our technology-oriented economy and be more geared to today's realities. A principal function of education must be to create a reserve of skilled, flexible and adaptable manpower. The knowledge explosion, changing social pressures and the demands of industry make it more necessary than ever to develop initiative, critical judgment, creative ability and powers of self-direction: all are qualities which modern educational practice seeks to develop and music has as important a contribution to make in this direction as any other subject.

The phenomenal developments in the mass media of communication have profound implications with regard to both leisure and taste and must therefore significantly influence the aims and methods of musical education. Technological and medical advances will increasingly result in people working fewer hours, retiring earlier and living longer. Society will thus become more and more a society of leisure and this trend will make an entirely new attitude to leisure all the more vital: as Sir Fred Clarke observed, the worst legacy of the Industrial Revolution was the vast gulf it opened up between work and life.[5] When our national economic problems become less acute, education for economic survival is likely to be replaced by education for creative leisure. The present unfortunate tendency of the mass media is to encourage passivity and increase the numbers of consumers and non-participants. However, the decline in amateur and domestic music-making need not continue indefinitely. People, with an increasing amount of spare time on their hands, may tire of being mere spectators and devote their energies to the acquisition of musical skills. Thus piano-smashing competitions may give way to a more constructive, creative use of leisure.

C. E. M. Joad warned of the power of the mass media to 'enfeeble the minds of the people, debauch their emotions and vulgarise their tastes'.[6] The ever-increasing availability of mechanically-reproduced music has resulted in the devaluing and cheapening of music's influence and the commercial evolution and high-pressure exploitation of new musical idioms have contributed to the creation of a sham, homogenized mass culture and to the dilution and standardization of tastes. Because of the quantity and accessibility of synthetic art and the fact that skilful and persuasive commercial techniques are directed at newly-affluent, highly-impressionable teen-agers, it is essential to refine and broaden tastes. Without discriminative ability and critical judgment, our pupils will become, according to Joad, 'raw material for manipulation by commercial pirates and domination by political adventurers'.

A further result of rapid technological advance is the gradual reduction in the time-span of usefulness of bodies of professional knowledge. This applies to teachers as well as doctors and scientists: with the broadening in scope of musical education and the developments in the technology of education, teachers will need to have skills in an increasing number of areas. They will need to be knowledgeable about methods of achieving a high standard of electronic reproduction of music, for one of the positive outcomes of sophisticated means of mass dissemination is an increasing demand for life-like reproduction. The advent of the gramophone helped to revolutionize certain branches of music in schools and such new audio-visual aids as colour television, electronic instruments and music blackboards, if skilfully used, may give a new dimension to musical education. Teachers will also need to keep abreast of developments in the field of computerized programmed learning, which will lead to an increasing mechanization of certain aspects of learning, and to be acquainted with such new educational techniques as that of team teaching.

FOREIGN EDUCATIONAL SYSTEMS

Since educational aims are so closely related to a society's particular needs and are a product of its unique character, educational organization and cultural heritage, it follows that systems and methods of education are not commodities which can be easily imported or exported, unless they lend themselves to considerable adaptation and modification; such adaptation, of course, involves much more than mere translation. In the nineteenth century, Hullah neglected this important educational principle when he attempted to import the system of G. L. B. Wilhem, who had been placed in charge of singing in the schools of Paris when music became a compulsory subject in 1835; Lowell Mason made an even more serious miscalculation when he introduced Kuebler's system into American schools. Curwen, on the other hand, was painstakingly careful in devising a system exactly suited to the needs of the state schools of his time. Curwen's tonic sol-fa system, of course, included very few original elements. His great achievement was to borrow and modify where necessary various English and continental methods and to weld them together into a coherent, integrated system of his own; tonic sol-fa thus incorporated features borrowed from Guido d'Arezzo's hexachordal system, Sarah Glover's modulator and movable doh systems, Lancashire sol-fa, Berneval's mental effects theory and the Paris–Galin–Chevé method.[7] In spite of the rivalry of Hullah, who was Inspector of Music in Training Colleges, Curwen's tonic sol-fa system revolutionized musical education in the state schools of this country and, even today, remains a uniquely effective method of aural training.

In view of the problems referred to in employing foreign educational methods, reference must be made to the work of the two leading composer–educationists of the twentieth century, Carl Orff and Zoltán Kodály. Their educational work, like their compositions, is the product of sharply contrasting social and artistic environments. *Orff-Schulwerk* had its origins in Orff's work at the Guentherschule, which he and Guenther established in Munich in 1924. Orff was anxious that music should not play a subordinate role to that of movement and so devised methods of improvisatory work which would enable musicians and dancers to exchange roles; with the help of Karl Maendler, he also developed instruments which would not demand so elaborate a technique as to inhibit creative enterprise. Orff's early experience in Munich and his work as a composer of operas and stage cantatas greatly influenced his educational work. The principal influences on Kodály's method of musical education were Hungarian folk music, on which he was a great authority, and the tonic sol-fa system, which he saw being taught in English schools. Kodály was perhaps more fortunate than Orff in getting his ideas generally accepted. The rise of Hitler prevented Orff and Gunild Keetman from introducing *Orff-Schulwerk* into Berlin primary schools and it was not until 1949, when he gave a series of broadcast lessons for schools, that Orff's active interest in *Schulwerk* was renewed. The Studio 49 factory was started by Klaus Becker, the five volumes of the revised *Orff-Schulwerk* were published between 1950 and 1954 and the Orff Institute, attached to the Mozarteum in Salzburg, was opened in 1963.

Kodály's *Choral Method*[8] does not require costly instruments or perhaps quite the same degree of sophisticated, creative musicianship on the part of the teachers as do the later stages of *Orff-Schulwerk*. It was largely Kodály's position as Hungary's most outstanding and revered composer which resulted in his educational work eventually receiving such enthusiastic state support. His publications were extensively used and a network of state music primary schools set up: over one hundred such schools have been established since 1950 and the pupils, aged six to fourteen, have six music lessons a week instead of the two in other schools. Thus in Hungary there was a nation-wide controlled situation which enabled the work of Kodály (and Curwen) to be put to the test in a way which has not been possible with *Orff-Schulwerk*. It may be argued, indeed, that it has been the widespread acceptance and implementation of Kodály's methods (apparently possible only in a totalitarian regime) rather than their great pedagogical originality that has been responsible for the dramatic transformation in the state of musical education in post-war Hungary.

It would be invidious, however, to attempt to compare the effectiveness of *Orff-Schulwerk* and Kodály's *Choral Method*. It is much more important to consider the extent to which they can be adapted to the needs of other countries. Two of the principal elements in the *Choral Method* are tonic sol-fa and Hungarian folk song and great emphasis is placed upon unaccompanied part-singing. Kodály's research into Hungarian folk music, like that of Bartók, began in 1905 and probed much more deeply than that of either Liszt or Erkel; it led him to conclude that the first musical language a child learns should be that of his own country. It would therefore be somewhat perverse to incorporate a great deal of Hungarian folk material into the music courses of children of other countries, where industrialization and urbanization may have destroyed the last remnants of a once dynamic folk culture. On the other hand, Kodály's systematic use of tonic sol-fa and such associated devices as modulators and hand-signs has led many teachers in other countries to reconsider the value and effectiveness of the tonic sol-fa system. *Orff-Schulwerk* is not a system in the sense that the *Choral Method* is, for the five volumes in no way constitute an *Urtext* to be practised and learnt. It possesses the necessary flexibility and adaptability to enable the compilers of the many foreign editions to use children's songs and nursery rhymes indigenous to their own countries.

CURRICULUM PLANNING

There are several broad principles underlying curriculum planning in music to which reference must be made. For instance, aims must be sufficiently precise and clearly-delineated to be capable of translation into terms of method and to form an adequate basis for purposes of evaluation. At the same time, they should not be so inflexible as to introduce rigidity into the teaching pro-gramme or to prevent adaptation to various changing circumstances. The music programme should be suffici-ently broadly-based and well-balanced to provide as wide a variety as possible of class and extra-curricular musical experiences and thus to cater for differing interests, abilities and aptitudes. It is important to ensure that there is an even balance between creative, executive and listen-ing activities. In the past, school music was accused of being too singing-centred and there is at present some risk of its becoming too instrument-centred. There is now an almost bewildering range of possible musical activities and materials from which to choose. The most comprehensive programme cannot possibly include all such activities or explore the entire range of musical literature; a well-balanced selection has to be made and, as far as possible, fused into an integrated whole.

In formulating aims in musical education, regard must be paid to the broader educational aims of the total school curriculum and a music programme must thus be planned in relation to the curriculum as a whole. Aims must also be conceived in terms of children's developing needs, interests and abilities and include provision for all-round personal development as well as the achievement of maximum musical potential.

'Music for every child, every child for music', which was the slogan adopted by the American Music Super-

visors' National Conference, succinctly expresses the
view shared by Orff, Kodály and Suzuki[9]: they have all
declared that the musical instinct is universal, that all
children possess innate musicianship in varying degrees
and that all are therefore potentially musical. Only misguided egalitarianism would deny the existence of individual differences in musical ability, attainment and maturity and the need to make adequate provision for them; on
the other hand, the view that music is an esoteric art-form
for which only a minority show any aptitude runs
contrary to current educational thought and ignores the
results of research into the nature and distribution of
musical ability.

A vital responsibility of teachers of music is to discover
exceptional latent talent and to provide the opportunity
for its optimum development. Although there are several
fee-paying schools with a strong musical bias and the
junior departments of the London colleges of music have
provided a valuable service for many years, it is frequently asserted that our educational system makes quite
inadequate provision for the location and fostering of
outstanding musical ability. During the post-war years,
however, many local education authorities have established junior music schools and over fifty of these are
now housed in well-staffed, well-equipped music centres.
At these centres there are facilities for tuition and practice, teachers' courses are held and opportunities are
provided for rehearsals and informal concerts by orchestras, choirs and vocal and instrumental ensembles. The
centres frequently house extensive music libraries and, by
providing a meeting-place for school and peripatetic
teachers as well as for teen-agers who have left school,
they can provide a focus for the varied musical activities
of an area.[10]

However, in spite of the work of such schools and centres and the development of youth orchestras and a range of vacation courses, many musicians are convinced that only the establishment of special, full-time music schools will adequately meet the needs of the exceptionally gifted. Such schools could be modelled on the Royal Ballet School, English cathedral choir schools, Belgian music schools (there are over two hundred such subsidized schools), Hungarian music primary schools, Russian ten-year music schools or the German, Austrian and Swiss *musische Gymnasien*. Two such schools in this country are the Central Tutorial School for Young Musicians, which was opened in 1962 with twenty pupils, aged six to eighteen, and the Yehudi Menuhin School, established at Stoke D'Abernon in the following year.[11] Advocates of special music schools rightly draw attention to the congested time-tables of ordinary schools and to the fact that early specialization in instrumental playing need not involve any neglect of general educational standards. Such schools, however, must of necessity be very costly small boarding schools, unless there is to be a possibly undesirable centralization of facilities and a somewhat standardized pattern of training. There is also the problem of adopting criteria for selection and it is important to remember that by no means all musically-gifted children wish to follow a professional career in music. Moreover, the notion of establishing special schools conflicts with the comprehensive, anti-segregational trend in current educational thought.

A school's music can perhaps best be judged by the provision it makes for those children with little obvious musical ability. Such children may include many of average and above general intelligence; because of such factors as a poor singing voice, limited previous musical

experience, lack of parental interest in music or a culturally-deprived environment, negative attitudes towards
music may have developed. In other cases, lack of musical
attainment may accompany general educational retardation. It is thus very difficult to make adequate provision
for the wide range of abilities, attainments and interests
represented in a large heterogeneous class. Group work
and a variety of extra-curricular musical activities may
help to some extent; setting, ability groupings and
additional optional courses may, however, be the only
real solution if children are to achieve their fullest
musical potential.

Reference was made in the previous chapter to some
of the ways in which music can contribute to the personal
development of mentally and physically-handicapped
children. Music can also contribute to raising the level
of functioning of slow learners if attention is given to
the use of methods and materials appropriate to their
needs and characteristics.[12] Thus slow learners are often
intellectually handicapped by limited powers of concentration and retention, and their reading ability is affected
by poor verbal comprehension. These factors restrict
progress in music, which involves tonal memory and
linguistic skills. It is therefore necessary to approach
music as an activity subject, in which group music-
making will cater for a wide range of aptitudes, use will
be made of straightforward, attractive songs featuring
verbal and musical repetition and suitable for learning by
rote, in which music for listening will be appropriate to
the children's limited span of attention and will be
presented with simple listening points, and in which
simple instruments and notational devices will enable
aural impressions to be reinforced by visual and kinaesthetic imagery.

For those children whose educational retardation is accompanied by emotional problems, music can serve as a channel for emotional release and catharsis. For such children, music can provide particularly valuable opportunities for creative and artistic self-expression via singing, playing, instrument-making, movement, mime and drama. It is not easy to find songs and instrumental works which, though technically-limited in their demands, are appropriate and acceptable in mood and character. The slow learner's intellectual and emotional problems may be aggravated by a culturally-impoverished home background; this is likely also to influence his response to music in view of the importance of social and environmental factors and of familiarity of musical idiom in determining musical attitudes and tastes.

Although it is obviously important to be aware of the limitations of slow learners, there has been a general tendency for their music lessons to be insufficiently demanding and extending. Attention must be given to discovering more dynamic approaches to music with the less able so that they can be challenged without being discouraged and be awakened to an awareness of their musical potential. In group music-making activities, they need not be constantly reminded of their verbal inadequacies. The development of new musical skills can lay the foundations of a possible leisure-time pursuit and contribute to a sense of achievement and adequacy: increased confidence and self-respect resulting from successful achievement can be vital factors in the formation of an integrated personality.

COGNITIVE AND AFFECTIVE AIMS

Many of the aims which teachers of music adopt are of a

cognitive nature. They include knowledge of the language and literature of music, judgment, conceptual understanding and musical skills. Other aims relate more to the feeling and emotional aspects of experience: such affective aims may be expressed in terms of attitudes, habits, sentiments, interests, appetites, values and beliefs. It is obvious that in a subject such as music there must be a judicious balance between cognitive and affective aims and objectives,[13] for neglect of, or undue emphasis on, any intellectual or emotional element will affect children's aesthetic response to music. Broad aims, involving a fusion of cognitive and affective elements, are likely to include musical appreciation, which in its broadest sense combines enjoyment, understanding and discrimination, and musical responsiveness. It is to the latter subject which we turn in the following chapter.

NOTES TO CHAPTER 2

1 Shuter, R., *The Psychology of Musical Ability*, Methuen, 1968.
2 Tovey, D. F., *Beethoven*, Oxford University Press, 1944.
3 Seashore, C. E., *The Psychology of Music*, New York: McGraw Hill, 1938.
Schoen, M., *The Psychology of Music*, New York: Ronald Press, 1940.
Lundin, R., *An Objective Psychology of Music*, New York: Ronald Press, 1967.
4 Silbermann, A., *The Sociology of Music*, Routledge & Kegan Paul, 1963.
5 Clarke, F., *Freedom in the Educative Society*, University of London Press, 1948.
6 Joad, C. E. M., *About Education*, Faber, 1945.
7 Rainbow, B., *The Land without Music*, Novello, 1967.
8 Szabó, H., *The Kodály Concept of Music Education*, Boosey & Hawkes, 1969.

9   Smith, H. F. A., 'Some Conclusions concerning the Suzuki Method of Teaching the Violin', *American String Teacher*, xv (1965), 1.
      Schultz, C., 'Shinichi Suzuki: the Genius of his Teaching', *American String Teacher*, xvi (1966), 1.

10   Standing Conference for Amateur Music, *Music Centres and the Training of Specially Talented Children*, National Council of Social Service, 1966.

11   Fenby, E., *Menuhin's House of Music*, Icon Books, 1968.

12   Dobbs, J. P. B., *The Slow Learner and Music*, Oxford University Press, 1966.

13   Bloom, B. S., *Taxonomy of Educational Objectives*, David McKay & Co., 1956.

3

MUSICAL RESPONSIVENESS

In order to broaden musical horizons, deepen insights and develop aesthetic awareness it is necessary to consider some of the principal factors determining musical responsiveness and their educational implications.

MUSICAL ABILITY

One of the most obvious factors is musical ability, the nature and measurement of which has occupied the attention of research workers more than any other aspect of musical education. Clerk Maxwell wrote of 'that Serbonian bog' between acoustics and music 'where whole armies of scientific musicians and musical men have sunk without filling it'[1] and, although half a century has elapsed since Carl Seashore first published his *Measures of Musical Talent*,[2] musical ability remains a subject of fierce controversy. Many musicians regard with distrust much of the work carried out in this field and query the musical credentials of those responsible for it; as Wing observes, the situation would be eased 'if the musician and psychologist were each sympathetic with, and cognizant of, the other's work and point of view'.[3]

Widely divergent views on the complex nature of musical ability are revealed in the various studies which have been made of measurement and evaluation. Some investigators subscribe to the atomistic or mosaic, multi-factor view that musical ability is a composite of several relatively independent, unrelated variables. Others argue that, since music involves patterns and relationships, it is more than the summation of its basic constituents; musical ability similarly is a unified phenomenon, a *Gestalt*, and therefore the character of the whole cannot be known simply from the study of its parts. The investigations of the unitary or omnibus theorists are based on the assumption that there is a general musical ability factor and a number of groups of inter-related abilities, arranged in hierarchical order. A further complication is the absence of generally-agreed criteria against which tests can be validated. Mursell,[4] unlike Seashore, favoured the use of external criteria and tests are now frequently validated in relation to musical proficiencies, use being made of teachers' assessments.

A criticism frequently levelled at Seashore's psycho-physical methods of investigating rudimentary auditory stimuli is their failure to make use of genuinely musical material. It is maintained that Seashore was excessively concerned with mere sensory, acoustical factors and that his measures are thus not musically oriented. It is certainly important to present tests in a truly musical context if light is to be thrown on the subjects' reactions to real musical situations. It is important also not to attempt to study musical phenomena without recognizing the dynamic inter-relationships of those phenomena.

Investigators working in the fields of general intelligence and musical ability have rightly emphasized the importance of genetic endowment; there has been a marked tendency, however, to underestimate the importance of environmental influences and, in regarding I.Q. and musical ability as innate, immutably fixed quantities, to adopt a somewhat pessimistic view of natural ceilings of ability. However, it is becoming increasingly recognized, as far as general ability is concerned, that linguistic inadequacy and poor academic attainment can be due as much to an unstimulating, culturally-deprived environment as to limited native endowment. Thus the Newsom Report, in emphasizing the need for all children to have an equal opportunity of 'acquiring' intelligence, denies that intelligence is a fixed quantum. It is clear that environmental factors alone cannot account for the achievements of musical prodigies or the wide range of musical attainments within a particular family. However, the view that musical ability is essentially an untrainable, unalterably fixed biological phenomenon ignores the importance of social and cultural determinants, the benefits of a rich musical environment and the effects of highly skilled teaching. The function of school music should not be to separate the musical sheep from the goats, but to give each child the opportunity to acquire musical intelligence. Even if the most stimulating musical environment cannot greatly affect the likelihood of musical achievement, it can certainly exert a powerful influence on musical interests, tastes, attitudes and habits. In this connection, it is interesting to note that only 75% of those accepted for entry to the Hungarian music primary schools pass the entrance aptitude test and that Suzuki is convinced that progress in music is determined, not by innate aptitude, but by environment and experience. Only by taking a more optimistic view of ceilings of musical ability and of what really imaginative and resourceful teaching can achieve can we hope to implement the policy of music for every child and every child for music.

Some tests of musical ability were designed because of the limited opportunities for instrumental instruction and the need to avoid unnecessary wastage. Several factors, in addition to that of innate capacity, are however of considerable importance. Parental interest and encouragement are essential as are those qualities of personality which are so difficult to measure scientifically: perseverance, determination, initiative, industriousness and enthusiasm are all necessary if the attractions of the increasing number of competing interests are to be resisted after the novelty of initial lessons has worn off. Physical attributes and skills are also highly relevant. They include motor control and co-ordination, manipulative facility and, in the case of wind players, lip and teeth formation.

Research has provided useful information about the distribution and sequential development of musical ability, disproving the notion that girls are, on average, more musical than boys, while confirming the importance of tonal memory in all types of musical activity and the need to make adequate and varied provision for the wide range of musical interests and aptitudes represented in an average class. Tests of ability are a useful aid to the early detection of above-average musical aptitude and, by indicating where particular strengths and weaknesses lie, can offer guidance in the choice of a suitable instrument for tuition. For reasons already discussed, the results of a test of musical ability should not be used as the sole determinant in selecting children for instrumental tuition, but be regarded as one source of information to supplement the teacher's own judgment: it must always be borne in mind that ability is a continuum and that, since ability tests[5] are intended by their designers to be treated as flexible instruments, caution and common sense are essential when interpreting results.

AESTHETIC SENSITIVITY

Most tests of musical ability are of a cognitive nature and do not claim to throw light on a subject's aesthetic capacity. Musicality, in its fullest sense, involves sympathetic emotional responsiveness to music as well as mere physical receptivity to sound, and cognitive tests are thus no more reliable a guide to musical sensitivity than are tests of vocal or instrumental ability. A few of the people working in the field of experimental aesthetics have studied the emotional response to music and attempted to devise tests of appreciative capacity and taste; such tests tend to measure achievement rather than innate capacity and consequently have poor validity and reliability. The fact that personality, temperament and emotional maturity may determine to a large extent the nature and extent of the aesthetic satisfaction derived from music influences the teacher's choice of music and accounts for the deepening of interest in music which often occurs during adolescent years. In this connection some interesting investigations have been made of possible links between musical preferences and tastes and the stability–neuroticism factor of personality.[6] The limited amount of significant research which has been conducted into the affective response to music leads one to assume that, because of the intangibility of music and the essentially subjective nature of the response to musical stimulus, aesthetic sensitivity and artistic sensibility do not lend themselves in the same way to scientific scrutiny

42

as do cognitive and perceptual factors, especially since they are largely unconscious processes and are influenced by such factors as intelligence, musical knowledge, understanding and skill, musicality, temperament and personality traits as well as by social and environmental considerations.

Our present limited knowledge of the nature and development of the affective response to music constitutes a serious handicap. In the case of highly-accomplished musicians, aesthetic sensibility is accompanied by cognitive efficiency. In many other instances, however, the two may be independent: thus aesthetic capacity may be masked by poor cognition while attitude and personality factors may prevent a person with musical ability, as measured by tests of sensory capacity, deriving aesthetic satisfaction from music. Restricted knowledge of, and research into, the affective response to music may be partially responsible for the inadequate emphasis placed on aesthetic values in music curriculum planning. Because of the complex problems of musical taste posed by the impact of mass media and the fact that the majority of our pupils will probably be consumers rather than performers of music, it is essential that more attention be given to studying the nature of aesthetic perception in music and its development in schools.

It is important in this connection that increased emphasis be placed upon developing awareness of, and responsiveness to, music's expressive range and upon making clear the expressive function of the raw materials and elements of music. Although the more subtle expressive devices and nuances, such as those involved in modulation and tonal contrast, require the existence of a rather more elaborate conceptual framework, quite young children can recognize the expressive significance

43

of the more obvious musical elements: tone, pitch, melodic line, interval and gradations, contrasts of tempo and dynamics, have similar expressive functions in both music and speech. Moreover, many expressive qualities of music can be explored and responded to through the corresponding qualities of movement. This approach enables children to grasp such expressive concepts as 'heavy', 'smooth', 'slow', 'high', and 'rhythmic'. One of the many merits of the tonic sol-fa system is the attention it gives, through such devices as hand signs, to the expressive effects of the degrees of the scale.

It is all too easy, when building a framework of musical concepts, to neglect the expressive role of those concepts. For instance, musical form is often very narrowly interpreted, excessive attention being given to pedantic dissection, syntax, formulae and formal strait-jackets. The study of musical form should be concerned with the organization of musical material, not mere descriptive labelling, divorced from context. It is unfortunate that so much that is written about musical form resembles the type of literary descriptive analysis parodied by Bernard Shaw:

> Shakespeare, dispensing with the customary exordium, announces his subject at once in the infinitive, in which mood it is presently repeated after a short connecting passage in which, brief as it is, we recognise the alternative and negative forms on which so much of the repetition depends. Here we reach a colon. . . .[7]

Walker's system of analysis, based on the unity of contrasting themes theory,[8] and Keller's wordless functional analysis, which involves the reconstruction of a score to bring out its latent unity, represent attempts to give due emphasis to the expressive function of musical form. It is also important to remember the inter-related nature of music's expressive elements, for the effects of intervals, dissonances, tonality, volume and timbre cannot be isolated from their musical context. Thus the effect of a major third in a work of Bach may be utterly different from that in a work of Schoenberg and a Mendelssohn Scherzo will disprove any generalizations about the emotive effects of minor keys.

Aesthetic awareness and sensitivity to music's expressive range can be most effectively developed through vocal and instrumental work. Expression, being structural rather than adhesive, is not something to be 'put in' after a piece has been learnt; neither will expressive concepts be properly established if interpretations are always imposed by the teacher. If singing is approached as a form of communication, children can better understand the need to project the mood of a song and convey its meaning. Much depends on the teacher's ability to set the mood and capture the children's imagination when introducing a song, and he must be able to explain the technical terms and references found in many traditional songs and sea shanties. Only by understanding the close relationship between the text and the music can children appreciate the expressive importance of tempo, phrasing, enunciation, rhythmic buoyancy, dynamics, tone and climaxes. It is also desirable to develop an awareness of appropriately expressive vocal colour: for instance, this will enable the children to project the contrast in mood between the third and fourth verses of 'Early one morning' and to convey the urgency of 'London's burning' and the mysterious quality of the final verses of 'Waltzing Mathilda' and Armstrong Gibbs's 'Five Eyes'. Attention should also be given to any descriptive effects in the piano accompaniment and the expressive role of the introduction, interludes and postlude.

Group music-making activities, which may involve devising an accompaniment to a song or background music for drama or mime, also provide valuable opportunities to develop an appreciation of music's expressive qualities. Children can exercise musical initiative and develop their discriminatory powers and sense of style by being encouraged to decide upon the type of accompaniment most suited to the expressive features of a song, the choice of instruments and the style of playing. Consideration should also be given to the dramatic and expressive functions of any sound effects used.

REACTION PATTERNS

A number of investigators have attempted to classify listeners according to their predominant response to music. The four reaction patterns which have most frequently emerged are the sensory, emotional, associative–imaginal and objective. The sensory response is explained by the closely connected psychological and physiological effects of music. In the case of the emotional response, the listener tends to project his feelings into the music which he may associate with particular human characteristics. The tendency for auditory and visual imagery to be aroused by music is responsible for a great deal of associative–imaginal listening. The fourth classification, objective, applies to the listener who describes his response in intellectual rather than subjective, emotional terms: thus he may comment on such features of a work as its craftsmanship, form, proportion and fitness, style and originality.

This type of investigation is open to several objections. The application of statistical methods to a random choice of subjects offers little guidance to the nature of aesthetic

appreciation. The choice of music was occasionally unsatisfactory in earlier investigations and too little account
has sometimes been taken of the duration of the quota-
tions, the quality of the interpretation, the listener's span
of attention, his familiarity with the idioms employed,
musical knowledge, understanding and skills, his prevail-
ing mood and the changes in his response to a piece of
music which may accompany increasing familiarity.
Moreover, since music is a non-verbal language and
aesthetic response to music is largely an unconscious
process, many adults find words inadequate to describe
their aesthetic experience and have recourse to a stereotyped response. It is therefore inadvisable to expect
young children to describe accurately or adequately their
response to a piece of music. Indeed, they may be able
to give expression to their response much more easily
and naturally through such creative outlets as art, movement and mime.

The fact that so much music heard in the classroom
has a programmatic or descriptive basis may perhaps be
attributed to the assumption that children's listening is
predominantly associative–imaginal. Tone poems, incidental and film music, operas, oratorios and ballet music
as well as programmatic overtures, symphonies, orchestral suites and solo items can serve as a springboard to
the imagination and stimulate work in movement, mime,
creative writing and art: for instance, children can design
an L.P. cover for a record of a piece of music with which
they are familiar. Subjects dealt with in programmatic
and descriptive music can be a means of linking together
different musical activities and provide useful opportunities for correlation with other subjects. Such central
themes may include nature, the seasons, seas and rivers,
animals, birds and insects, towns and countries, national

47

legends, Shakespearian plays, paintings and portraits, machinery, magic and the supernatural. In the case of certain programmatic works, some knowledge of the story may be necessary to create an appropriate mood and channel the listener's thoughts; in other cases even a knowledge of the title of a work may be unnecessary for understanding and enjoyment, especially if it is an unauthorized addition by a publisher. Because of music's flexibility, the imagery aroused by a piece of music can vary considerably between listeners. By describing in detail what a piece of music is 'about', the teacher is not allowing the imagination free play and is preventing subjective interpretations. There is a common tendency to exaggerate children's need for verbal descriptions of the meaning of music. An excessive concern with extra-musical factors can distract attention from the music itself and, in the long run, encourage the idea that all music describes scenes or events.

MUSICAL KNOWLEDGE

Responsiveness to music is obviously influenced to a considerable extent by one's knowledge and under-standing of the language and literature of music and one's creative, executive and listening skills. Musical respon-siveness is a matter of feeling as well as knowing and the possession of musical knowledge, skills and proficiencies does not necessarily imply also the possession of aesthetic receptiveness and taste. Some writers have tended to overestimate the validity of the intellectual at the expense of the emotional response: thus Hanslick[9] denied the relevance of emotion in 'pure listening' and Révész[10] has declared that 'not emotion, enthusiasm, love of music, a warm interest in it, but the mental conquest of music as an art characterises the musical person'. It is unrealistic, however, to attempt to differentiate sharply between music's intellectual and emotional effects, for the mind and emotions do not function independently. Thus the total effect of any work of art is much more than the sum of the effects of its constituent elements, for they interact and merge into a formal unity. Interpretative insight and knowledge and appreciation of such qualities as originality, craftsmanship and style can clarify music's affective meaning, enhance and enrich the listener's emotional response and, as Stockhausen has observed, 'smooth the way to feeling'.

The creation of a framework of musical concepts and the development of skills are subjects which will be dealt with in subsequent chapters. Our present concern is with knowledge of the literature of music. One of the principal aims of music education must be to preserve and transmit our rich musical heritage by acquainting children with representative examples of man's finest musical achievements and by making clear their relationship to our total cultural inheritance. It must be emphasized at the outset that 'educational' music, in the worst sense of the term, forms no part of this musical heritage. Kodály declared that we must get rid of 'the pedagogical superstition that only some diluted substitute art is suitable for teaching material'. Educational music, to which such adjectives as faded, devitalized, anaemic and antiseptic have frequently been applied, represents an unfortunate carry-over from the songs specially manufactured for children during the nineteenth century. Perhaps the worst features of 'educational' songs are their poor words (the teacher has to be wary in this respect also of certain translations of Bach and Handel), their derivative, stilted melodic lines, their want of rhythmic interest and their unstylistic accompani-

49

ments. Also to be avoided are arrangements which destroy the integrity of a composer's conception and outmoded material, devoid of musical quality and interest, intended for use in instrumental instruction. The use of such music is clearly conducive to the development of neither aesthetic sensitivity nor taste and judgment. The great virtue of the educational music of Orff and Kodály is that neither composer has ever lapsed into musical baby-talk: *Schulwerk* and *Carmina Burana* have the same underlying artistic principles, as do the *Choral Method* and *Psalmus Hungaricus*.

As far as possible children's knowledge of the literature of music should be gained at first hand through their own performances. This necessitates selecting music suited to their stage of musical growth and experience: thus in choosing songs regard has to be paid to compass, vocal line, phrase structure and rhythmic complexities. Through class singing a repertoire can be built up of traditional and folk songs of various nations, including nursery rhymes, cumulative and dialogue songs, shanties, work songs, spirituals and carols, as well as rounds, canons and classical and modern part-songs. Adverse comments have frequently been made about the poor quality of music making in morning assembly; however the use of more appropriate hymns, the Gelineau psalm-settings and contributions by small instrumental ensembles may help to revitalize music in assembly.

School choirs, whether they be unison, two-part, S.S.A., S.A.B., S.A.T.B., or T.T.B.B., provide a splendid opportunity to explore the choral repertoire. Indeed, because of such problems as weak string sections and incomplete wind sections, the average school orchestra cannot be nearly as adventurous and ambitious in its choice of works as the average choir. Although there is a wealth of choral music available, the number of suitable extended secular works is however somewhat limited. Members of choirs may have the additional opportunity to take part in operatic productions. Several ballad operas and adaptations of operas by Handel, Gluck, Mozart and Rossini have been published; many schools have also given performances of operas by composers ranging in time from Purcell to Britten. Selected members of school choirs can specialize in the performance of ayres, balletts, canzonets and madrigals as well as modern part-songs.

Changes in methods of editing music for school orchestras have reflected the changing scope of school orchestral playing. Thus the wind parts in older editions are too elementary and uninteresting for present-day wind players. Publishers now cater for most exigencies: there are series of works flexibly scored for all possible permutations of instrumental availability, works with a bias towards the wind section, finely-graded works with parts for players of widely-differing attainments, works including parts for a motley collection of non-orchestral instruments as well as specially-commissioned works in modern idioms.

Although there are only a quarter of the number of adult brass bands that there were before the war, the brass band movement in schools is flourishing. This is partly due to the fact that more rapid progress can be made in the initial stages of learning brass instruments, and many boys regard band instruments as more attractively 'virile' than orchestral instruments; a brass band may range in size from one comprising two B flat cornets, an E flat tenor horn and a B flat euphonium to a complete band of twenty-five brass players plus percussion. Brass bands have been frequently criticized for their reluctance to explore the band repertoire, which extends from the music of Gabrieli to specially-written works by Elgar, Holst and Howells. Although much orchestral music cannot easily be arranged for school brass bands because of the problems involved in adapting string parts, motets and appropriate organ works can be effective for this purpose.

The balance between the numbers of children learning wind and stringed instruments has altered to such an extent that, in some schools, it is not possible for all the wind players to perform regularly in the school orchestra. Wind ensembles are therefore assuming increasing importance. Brass trios (two trumpets and horn), quartets (two trumpets, trombone and horn), and woodwind quintets (four woodwind plus horn) can explore the wide range of music which is being published for them. Military and symphonic bands can also make valuable provision for wind players, especially since over half the instruments required for such bands are already possessed by complete school orchestras. Additional ensemble experience can be provided by the formation of recorder consorts, guitar groups, for which much music is currently being published, and chamber duos, trios and quartets.

Thus, as stated earlier, acquaintance with our musical heritage can be gained at first hand through performance by the pupils. The statement, however, needs amplification. Firstly, to limit the music studied to works the children are technically capable of performing would place an absurdly unnecessary restriction on their range of musical activities and would ignore the value of experiences gained through listening and movement. Secondly, the transmission of our musical heritage can form too narrow and inadequate a basis for musical education: Mursell condemned the excessive emphasis placed on folk song and a vocal repertoire based on English folk songs would clearly be inappropriate for schools with a large proportion of immigrants.

CONTEMPORARY MUSIC

A special danger of concentrating on past cultural achievements is that it can lead to a serious neglect of contemporary music. It has been stated with great truth that a society in which contemporary art is not encouraged 'deserves the artistic sterility which will almost certainly result'. The alarming widening of the composer–audience gap has been attributed to the preoccupation of many avant-garde composers with experimentation and their take-it-or-leave-it attitude towards the need for communication; the gap is also due to the narrow, conservative tastes of the concert-going public. Examining boards, however, are at last recognizing the importance of developing interest in and understanding of twentieth-century idioms. School music, too, can counteract the view that music is a static art form and that all serious composers are dead composers.

Virtually all the music that children listen to and perform is rooted in the diatonic system, as is the tonic sol-fa system, with its emphasis on developing a sense of tonality. Indeed, it may be argued that such tonality-dominated musical experiences restrict the capacity of children to appreciate a great deal of the music composed during the last half-century and that the fixed-doh system is more appropriate to modern tonally-anchorless music. Whatever the validity of such arguments, there is ample evidence to suggest that group improvisatory activities can enable experiments to be made with various non-diatonic systems and provide some insight into the creative processes of contemporary music. Children can thus be introduced to polytonal, atonal and microtonal music and gain some understanding, for instance, of Stravinsky's use of ostinati and Webern's use of fragmented motives and palindrome procedures. Still more recently evolved techniques, associated with such composers as Cage, Stockhausen, Berio and Penderecki, lend themselves particularly well to group improvisatory work. These composers are sensitively exploring new sound qualities, timbres, densities and textures and their use of aleatoric or chance devices and flexible notation demands of the performer a degree of creative imagination comparable to that demanded of the performer in the eighteenth century. These trends have led to some interesting experimental work with children, in which they explore the expressive range of sounds that can be obtained from varied sound-producing materials as well as conventional instruments and in which use is made of graphic, diagrammatic and outline scores[11] for purposes of both performance and composition. With the aid of a tape recorder, children can explore still further the world of sound and be introduced to electronic music and *musique concrète*; experiments in this field involve the manipulation of volume and speed controls, superimposition and the use of loop recorders, contact microphones and sound-generating circuits.

Experimental work of the type referred to above is likely to be impatiently dismissed by many teachers as time-consuming gimmickry indulged in by composer–teachers in search of publicity. This is particularly likely to be so in the case of those teachers who equate all avant-garde music with the indiscriminate hurling of pots of paint at canvases. In fact, if skilfully approached, such work can develop a highly-sensitive awareness of the expressive possibilities of sound and habits of concentrated listening and provide an added dimension to creative music in schools. The problem of shortage of time is of course a serious one and the argument that the music curriculum should be entirely contemporary has to be dismissed, if only for the reason that an understanding of the twentieth-century tonal revolution depends to a very great extent on a knowledge of what led up to it.

JAZZ

No discussion of twentieth-century music would be complete without some reference to jazz.[12] Some teachers introduce jazz into their lessons, not because they are convinced of its intrinsic importance and musical qualities, but because they see in it an opportunity to meet half-way the enormous enthusiasm of teen-agers for 'pop' music. This approach is somewhat misguided for, although jazz and 'pop' are sometimes used as interchangeable terms, traditional jazz and current 'pop' idioms have very little in common. Moreover, the once-popular jazz-versus-classics debates served very little purpose. Indeed, they may have done positive harm by unnecessarily creating barriers between different types of music. It has been estimated that there are over six thousand jazz bands in American high schools; in this country Dr Donald Hughes has done valuable pioneer work in developing a discriminating, informed interest in jazz amongst young people and, more recently, the London Schools' Jazz Orchestra and the Jazz Association have been formed.

Various methods of approach can be adopted towards the study of jazz, either in class lessons or music society meetings. One of the most common approaches involves a study of the history of jazz in relation to its social background. Jazz is essentially a hybrid form, having its roots in African music but also incorporating elements borrowed from such diverse sources as American traditional songs and war marches, hymn tunes and Spanish and French dances. Jazz developed, particularly during the period following the emancipation of the slaves, and Dixieland bands had their origin in the Negro marching bands of New Orleans which played at parades and funerals; improvisatory methods, within a prescribed rhythmic and harmonic framework, were evolved and new styles of playing the cornet, clarinet and trombone which were developed were greatly influenced by Negro styles of singing. After the First World War enthusiasm for jazz spread northwards to Chicago and, in the 1920s, to Europe also. The era of true traditional jazz ended soon after the Wall Street Crash and was followed by the emergence of the big swing bands in the 1930s. The impact of jazz at this time is evident in the music of several serious composers, including Lambert, Walton, Copland, Ravel, Hindemith and Stravinsky; Gershwin and Liebermann attempted to combine symphonic and jazz elements, but perhaps only Milhaud succeeded fully in this endeavour.

Useful comparisons may be made between jazz and earlier musical forms and styles of playing. The three-phrase blues formula may be compared with the passamezzo and the boogie-woogie bass with the ground, chaconne and passacaglia. Jazz has several features in common with baroque music: the notation of both is necessarily imprecise because of the considerable improvisatory element, and the role of the banjo and double bass is similar to that of continuo instruments.

These baroque elements in jazz explain the current enthusiasm for vocal and instrumental jazz treatments of the music of Bach and his contemporaries. Moreover the musicological research conducted into *Aufführungspraxis* has something in common with the equally earnest and painstaking investigations into, and the attempts to re-create, the authentic New Orleans style. Jazz can throw additional light on the true nature of tempo rubato; a study of chamber music can include recordings by the Venuti–Lang Duo and the small ensembles of Goodman; keyboard virtuosity can be illustrated by reference to the transcriptions of both Vladimir Horowitz and Art Tatum; anti-romantic and neo-classicist trends can be discerned in the music of the West Coast School of the 1950s; and certain avant-garde techniques can be observed in the music of such men as Kenton and Gillespie.

ATTITUDE AND TASTE

Success in the teaching of such subjects as music depends as much on creating favourable dispositions and positive, constructive attitudes as on imparting information and developing skills. The establishment of constructive attitudes towards music determines the quality and efficiency of musical learning and is vital if the foundations are to be laid of a taste for, as well as taste in music. The build-up of negative attitudes and prejudices is attributable to many complex factors, the most obvious being boredom and a sense of irrelevance and aimlessness in the teaching. A teacher whose predecessor lacked skill and authority in the classroom and who relied heavily on educational music of the worst sort will require considerable resourcefulness and patience if he is to improve the image of music in his school. Negative attitudes, which can be highly infectious, are also acquired through persistent failure. Thus lack of progress in learning to play an instrument or lack of aptitude for singing can have a harmful effect on a child's attitude to music as a whole. Destructive attitudes can also develop during the adolescent years when boys' voices are changing and enthusiasms for 'pop' music are developing. It is during these years also that culturally-induced prejudices against serious music can grow. Unfortunate nomenclature does not help—high-brow, classical, serious, straight, non-pop (un-pop ?)—and, as suggested earlier, neglect of modern music can give the impression that school music is a fossilized, antiquarian art-form, with musty museum associations.

It is fortunate that, since they are acquired habits of thought, attitudes and tastes are modifiable. Although occasionally a single event or experience can have a transforming effect on attitude, the creation of positive, constructive attitudes is generally a cumulative process. Favourable attitudes result from favourable experiences and are thus the product of conditioning: although it has acquired sinister overtones, conditioning is a basic factor in learning processes. A healthy musical climate is all-important and a stimulating physical and social environment, in which pupils are actively involved and are helped to create their own standards of musical values, is likely to generate positive attitudes and tastes. A music room should have an aesthetically pleasing appearance and there should be no ugly visual or auditory distractions. The condition of equipment and books is important and display material should not be excessive or remain unchanged for long periods; reproductions of paintings with musical themes, such as those of Vermeer and Renoir, can greatly enhance the appearance of a music room.

The most important factors in creating a stimulating environment are the personality and skill of the teacher. Children are highly impressionable and the personal qualities of the teacher are especially important in aesthetic education: hence the need for reciprocal respect and a community of feeling between a teacher and his pupils. The teacher is not a colourless medium and the qualities of vitality and sincerity and the ability to communicate enthusiasm count for a great deal. On the other hand insincere, rapturous enthusiasm will be sensed immediately by the pupils and the offending teacher will either be regarded with amused tolerance or be dismissed as a crank. Musical integrity is also a powerful factor and the conscientious teacher will continue to develop his knowledge and skills and extend his interests. He will keep abreast of educational developments and take part in a varied range of musical activities. These may include attendance at music teachers' courses and workshops and membership of choirs, orchestras and chamber ensembles. In many ways, then, the personal and musical qualities required of a teacher are not so very unlike those required of a concert performer.

As far as classroom skills are concerned, the successful teacher will recognize the importance of intrinsic motivation and the roles of interest and achievement in building up favourable attitudes. Interest and curiosity, which can be canalized into channels of knowledge, understanding and skills, are dependent on the work being meaningful, appropriate to the pupils' level of intellectual, emotional and physical maturation, relevant to their needs and systematically presented. Positive incentives and encouragement are also of vital importance. Fault-finding, nagging, punishment and similar examples of negative reinforcement may influence effort but inhibit the development of positive attitudes; similarly such examples of extrinsic motivation as preparation for examinations will not necessarily ensure continued musical interest and initiative. Achievement, like praise, is an important secondary reinforcer. Children need to be challenged, without being over-stretched, and goals must therefore constantly be moved forward, without becoming completely out of reach. Since children need to experience the satisfaction of success and achievement, it is important to provide varied opportunities for the acquisition of creative, linguistic, executive and listening skills through active involvement and participation. It is undoubtedly true that the creation of constructive attitudes must be based upon pleasurable experiences. This does not mean, however, that school music must be an undemanding form of entertainment and that low standards of work and performance must be accepted. A business-like, purposeful approach to music achieves the most satisfactory results and it is wrong to assume that an insistence on high standards, whether they be of recorder playing or of vocal tone and intonation, will result in the development of negative attitudes towards music.

Familiarity and habituation are important factors in determining attitude and taste. There is much truth in the saying 'familiarity begets affection': liking depends on familiarity and dislike has its roots in fear of the unknown. As far as music is concerned, people do not appear to be curious about and interested in the unknown. They like what they know, although they insist that they know what they like. Even the range of interests of regular concert-goers is restricted to the type of music of which they have had experience. Thus they are likely to be enthusiastic about nineteenth-century orchestral music but have negligible interest in fifteenth-century or oriental music. Similarly many members of choirs rarely attend orchestral concerts. It follows therefore that the argument that singing alone is an adequate basis for school music is quite fallacious: opportunities must be provided for children to receive as wide a range of musical experiences as possible.

The importance of familiarity and habituation also points to the need for controlled and systematic repetition. First hearings often make little impression. Indeed the initial reaction may be quite unfavourable. Even the 'pop' music industry relies heavily upon 'plugging' and 'exposure' and the large number of enquiries made about musical items used regularly as signature tunes in broadcasts illustrates the considerable change in response and enjoyment which can accompany repetition and increasing familiarity. These are examples, not only of the application of Gestalt psychology, but also of the cultural conditioning achieved by the mass media and their power to set standards of taste.

Results of research conducted into attitudes towards music and into the relationship between taste and socio-economic status confirm that attitudes and tastes are not absolute, but are culturally and environmentally determined.[13] Standards of taste therefore cannot be arbitrarily imposed. Children can be enticed but not wrenched away from mediocrity. People's beliefs, prejudices, attitudes and tastes are the products of their immediate environment. The fact that the rigid class distinctions which formerly characterized our society were accompanied by equally rigid cultural distinctions may explain the tendency to associate certain artistic pursuits, like certain sports and games, with particular socio-economic groups. Thus pop music and soccer are likely to be placed in one group and Glyndebourne opera, chamber music and croquet in another. Music's association with the system of aristocratic patronage may have been initially responsible for such prejudices. The nationalist movement and the folk song revival in the nineteenth century helped to weaken music's socio-economic associations; in recent years the Proms have had the same effect, and it is unfortunate that the B.B.C's four radio channels served to reinforce harmful and meaningless cultural demarcations.

'POP' MUSIC

The appeal of 'pop' music to teen-agers may be explained by the prejudicial effects of social and environmental factors.[14] The musical tastes of the immature are conditioned very much by prejudice and fashion, and the uniform tastes in 'pop' music may be regarded as a manifestation of young people's gregarious instinct, their desire to be accepted by the group and their fear of cultural isolation. Adolescent affluence and independence are comparatively recent phenomena and have coincided with a period of remarkable development in the mass media of communication; commercial interests have been very quick to take advantage of this state of affairs and, by the use of skilful techniques of promotion, advertising and exposure, have successfully exploited adolescent affluence and susceptibility. As far as teachers are concerned, it is the quantity of 'pop' music which constitutes an even more serious problem than its quality and which reinforces the need for a richly varied counterbalancing range of musical experiences in schools. This is not to imply that the quality of all 'pop' music is poor or that its effects are necessarily deplorable. Indeed some contemporary 'pop' music has considerable musical interest. Many adults condemn its crudely erotic appeal and it is true that the remarkable hypnotic power of certain male 'pop' singers to induce sexual ecstasy in the girls in their audiences would appear to confirm Freud's belief that 'the concept of the beautiful is rooted in the soil of sexual excitement'! However, less articulate teen-agers can find in the convulsive, relentless beat of 'pop' music a possibly useful emotional outlet for the frustrations and stresses of adolescence. 'Pop' music provides striking evidence of music's liberating capacity and the degree of communication achieved is often remarkable.

The generation gap prevents adults fully comprehending the nature and appeal of 'pop' music, for it is a jealously-guarded sub-culture. Some teachers adopt such a hostile attitude towards 'pop' music that one is tempted to believe that they would insist on their music rooms being reconsecrated if ever such music were to be played there! These teachers maintain that any attempt to build on a taste for an essentially synthetic culture would be equivalent to using pornography as a basis for the development of literary taste. Other teachers argue that, because of the problems of apathy and the prejudice against serious music, 'pop' music can be used as a starting point in order to canalize young people's frenzied enthusiasms for such music into more constructive channels, to proceed from the known to the unknown, to illustrate the basic principles underlying all music and thereby to remove harmful barriers in children's minds between 'pop' and other types of music. It is true that much is to be gained from a study of the elements in 'pop' music which contribute to its appeal. They include, for example, duple rhythms, repetition, melodies of limited range, unusual timbres and live performance. It is also important to break through barriers of prejudice, where they exist, and to avoid adopting a policy which will serve only to strengthen negative attitudes. However, the introduction of 'pop' music into class lessons poses serious problems. Unless it can be developed upon, 'pop' music represents an educational cul-de-sac; musical education is concerned with growth and development, not the promotion of trivia, and there is a danger of simply pandering to and reinforcing existing tastes instead of extending and broadening them.

THE LANGUAGE OF MUSIC

Widely differing theories have been held about music as a language of the emotions. There was, for instance, the doctrine of the affections (*Affektenlehre*), which so dominated musical thought in the seventeenth and eighteenth centuries. The French Encyclopaedists, who subscribed to the doctrine, constantly referred to the need for music to 'paint' and be emotionally precise, and therefore held the view that music was at its best when allied to words. Such musicians as Avison and Mattheson[15] believed that the various affections could be classified and that specific styles and instruments could be associated with each of them. Although he does not subscribe to so naive a philosophy, Deryck Cooke[16] asserts that music is a much more precise language of the emotions than is generally realized and he has sought to show how all composers whose music has a tonal basis have used the same basic musical vocabulary to express and evoke particular emotions, and how musical expression is achieved by a composer's colouring the vitalizing agents of volume, time and intervallic tension by the characterizing agents of tone-colour and texture. At the other extreme is the view of Stravinsky, who has contended that music is neither a language nor a communication of emotions since it is incapable of expressing anything; *Gebrauchs-musik*, on the other hand, may be regarded as an expression of the belief in music as a means of communication, and of the concern at the alleged breakdown in communication between many twentieth-century composers and their audiences.

In spite of such markedly-differing views on the precision of the language of music, it is clear that the wide variety of factors influencing musical responsiveness is responsible for the remarkable diversity of people's reactions to music. A piece of music can stimulate a wide range of feelings, moods and imagery in a group of listeners and the flexibility of music enables each listener to draw on it according to his emotional and intellectual needs. Even in the case of music with a definite programmatic basis, investigations have revealed that the majority of listeners are unable to identify with any degree of precision the events or moods the composer intended to portray or convey and they have drawn attention to the strictly limited imitative and descriptive capacities of what is essentially a non-articulate language. The fact that the response to a musical stimulus is a highly subjective mental phenomenon may reasonably lead one to assume that many of the characteristics applied to music would be more accurately ascribed to a listener's response and that musical beauty thus resides in the ear of the beholder, rather than in the music itself. Some would go still further and contend that there can be no objective, absolute standards of musical taste. They would perhaps cite Brahms's dislike of the music of Bruckner, Wolf's of Brahms and Debussy's of Gluck and Berlioz to support their argument.

Even if one is not prepared to subscribe to such a view, it must be acknowledged that, for instance, the changing attitude towards dissonance clearly illustrates the importance of the individual listener's response to an art form which is utterly dependent on re-creation and which has so many links in its complex chain of communication. Because of the subjective nature of the response to music, it has been said that musical appreciation, in its fullest sense, has to be caught, not taught, and that it is more accurate to speak of teaching for musical appreciation than of teaching appreciation itself. To achieve this end, it is necessary to develop responsiveness to music as a source of enjoyment and a means of expression, to foster aesthetic awareness and positive attitudes, to create, as well as satisfy, needs, appetites and interests and to make possible continued independent musical growth and development by extending knowledge and understanding of the language and literature of music. The possession of a conceptual framework and varied skills can considerably influence the quality of musical responsiveness and it is to a study of these subjects that the following chapters are devoted.

NOTES TO CHAPTER 3

1 Lowery, H., *The Background of Music*, Hutchinson's University Library, 1952.

2 Seashore, C. E., Lewis, D., Saetveit, J. G., *Seashore Measures of Musical Talent*, New York: Psychological Corporation, rev. 1960.

3 Wing, H. D., *Tests of Musical Ability and Appreciation*, Cambridge University Press, 2nd edition, 1968.

4 Mursell, J. L., *The Psychology of Music*, New York: Norton & Co., 1937.

5 Gordon, E., *Musical Aptitude Profile*, Boston: Houghton Mifflin Co., 1965.

Bentley, A., *Measures of Musical Abilities*, Harrap Audio-Visual Aids, 1966.

6   Payne, E., 'Musical Taste and Personality', *British Journal of Psychology*, lviii (1967), 1-2 and 133-138).

7   Shenfield, M., 'Shaw as Music Critic', *Music & Letters*, xxxix (1958), No. 4.

8   Walker, A., *A Study in Musical Analysis*, Barrie & Rockliff, 1962.

9   Hanslick, E., *The Beautiful in Music*, Novello, 1891.

10 Révész, F., *Introduction to the Psychology of Music*, Longmans, 1953.

11 Self, G., *New Sounds in Class*, Universal Edition, 1967.

12 Dankworth, A., *Jazz: an Introduction to its Musical Basis*, Oxford University Press, 1968.

13 Farnsworth, P. R., *The Social Psychology of Music*, Holt, Rinehart & Winston, 1958.

14 Swanwick, K., *Popular Music and the Teacher*, Pergamon, 1968.
    Mabey, R., *The Pop Process*, Hutchinson Educational, 1969.

15 Avison, C., *An Essay on Musical Expression*, London: C. Davis, 1752.
    Mattheson, J., *Das Neu-Eröffnete Orchestre*, Hamburg, 1713, i. 266.

16 Cooke, D., *The Language of Music*, Oxford University Press, 1959.

4

UNDERSTANDING

Musical understanding is developed by helping children to organize their experiences in creative and linguistic work, vocal and instrumental performance, movement and listening in order to create a framework of musical concepts. Some of the more obvious basic concepts include the items listed below.

Sound

Some of the recent developments in music, referred to in the previous chapter, have served to emphasize the narrowness and inadequacy of conventional dictionary definitions of the term 'music'. Children need to investigate the phenomena of sound patterns and relationships and become increasingly aware of the familiar sounds of their environment, of the musical qualities of various sound-producing materials and of the expressive range of sounds which can be produced by instruments and voices.

Rhythm

Pulse, pulse groupings and pattern (equal and unequal subdivisions of pulse).

Pitch

Direction (high–low, up–down–same), intervals (step–leap, relative size of leaps, interval recognition), pattern (scale-wise, chordal, sequential and other common configurations) and tonal organization (modal, pentatonic, major, minor, chromatic, whole-tone and dodecaphonic scales, modulation, tonality, polytonality, atonality and microtonality).

Harmony

Melodic and harmonic intervals, consonance and dissonance, tonality, cadence, primary and secondary chord qualities and characteristics.

Form

Rhythmic and melodic germ-cells and motives, phrase structure (balance and antithesis), repetition, contrast and variation.

Style

Period and regional, individual composers' styles and the relationship to styles of other art-forms.

Concepts of tempo, timbre, dynamics and texture also contribute to an awareness and appreciation of the expressive range of music.

MUSICAL EXPERIENCE

Each concept should be explored through a range of musically meaningful activities. Thus in dealing with formal concepts, antiphonal singing of balancing phrases in such dialogue songs as 'The deaf woman's courtship' can help to develop an awareness of phrase structure; repetitions, similarities, differences and contrasts can be identified in copies of songs, question and answer phrases and rondo structures can form the basis of creative work and both devising accompaniments and moving to music provide opportunities to observe such features as contrast and repetition. Concepts should always be presented in a genuinely musical context, for the constituents of music cannot be studied in isolation. The perfect fourth, for example, depends for its effect on its context: even in the pentatonic scale[1] there are four such intervals. Familiar song material provides the most obvious means of establishing a basic musical vocabulary. The notes of the primary chords, for instance, can be studied in this way and sol-fa syllables can be introduced in association with phrases from familiar songs.

Learning is essentially a creative process which emerges from immediate, assimilative experience. Knowledge, concepts and skills are best acquired incidentally in the course of varied, musically-educative experience and practical, purposeful activity. The child is the agent of his own learning and the emphasis must therefore be on active self-involvement and first-hand experience. Gramophone records, like pictures and diagrams, are at best only substitutes for such experience.

Young children learn a great deal through spontaneous, undirected play and their early musical experiences can thus be related to the informal and spontaneous musical activities in which they take part. Indeed the process of musical growth has its roots in the finger play songs, singing games and rhythmic movements which feature in children's regular play activities. Carl Orff exploits the close association between education and play in his use of the notes me, soh and lah, for the falling third and rising fourth are used instinctively in the natural chants of early childhood; they also form the basis of the victorious chants of football supporters. In *Orff-Schulwerk*, the falling third is introduced in association with name-calling, street cries and songs and is used for vocal and instrumental patterning and questions and answers. The note 'lah' is added and the three-note germ-cell is similarly used for patterning and questions and answers as well as for forming a basis of improvised settings of simple jingles.

Conceptual growth is achieved, not by coaching, drilling and listing facts to be memorized, but by providing exploratory and investigative experiences and developing powers of initiative and self-direction. Insight into the nature of sound, for instance, can be gained by means of enquiry, exploration, experimentation and self-discovery. There has been a tendency in the past to neglect general auditory awareness in education and the instruction 'look at' has figured much more prominently than 'listen to'. Children should be encouraged to be aurally alert to the familiar, everyday sounds of their environment.[2] Their attention can be directed to such natural sounds as those of the sea, rivers, rain, thunder, wind, animals and birds; man-made sounds of definite and indefinite pitch may be associated with vehicles, trains, ships and aeroplanes, circular saws, steam kettles, bells, music boxes, barrel organs, klaxons, the signals of television channels and the chimes of clocks and ice-cream vans. Recorded sounds and pictures can be used to stimulate the children's aural imagination and they can be encouraged to recognize, imitate or imagine the sounds associated with a fairground, a street market, a nineteenth-century street, a forest at night or a church yard. A study of the imitative possibilities and limitations of musical instruments, voices and familiar sound-producing materials can be associated with the use of expressive, dramatic and colouristic sound effects in song and poetry accompaniments and background music for stories, mime and drama; it can also be linked with a study of programme music. Simple practical experiments can be carried out, using familiar objects as sound-producing mechanisms; the distinction between noise and music can be examined, as can children's attempts to define the term 'music'. The expressive tonal range of conventional musical instruments should also be fully explored: experiments should be made in playing drums and tuned percussion instruments with different headed beaters, the grand effect of clashed cymbals should be compared with the *misterioso* effect of a cymbal struck with a soft beater and different ways of playing such instruments as tambours, tambourines and triangles should be explored.

Investigative experiences and the making of simple instruments can be associated with a study of the principles of elementary acoustics. The three characteristics of sound are pitch, intensity and timbre. By experimenting with such simple vibrating agencies as elastic bands, comb and paper and rulers under desk-lids, children can learn, through hearing, seeing and feeling, that pitch is determined by the frequency of vibrations and intensity by their amplitude. Children can also investigate the effects on pitch of varying quantities of water being poured into glass tumblers, and a tube, mouthpiece and funnel can be used to illustrate the principles of the harmonic series of brass instruments. Audiospectrometers have been used to show how changes in timbre are caused by changes in the pattern of harmonics. In the case of older children, the exploration of sound can be linked to experimental work carried out in the physics lessons. The more advanced study of acoustics can include investigations into the transmission and reception of sound. The standard experiment with an electric bell and bell jar may be used to demonstrate the fact that air carries sound, and other sound-transmitting media can also be investigated. Other topics can include the structure of the ear and the range of audibility, the acoustics of rooms and buildings and the speed of sound, and the classification of instruments according to their generators, vibrators and resonators. An exploration of new sound patterns can take in a study of electronic production, reproduction and distortion of sound, and an investigation into the development of gramophone recording can form the basis of an interesting project.

Pitch concepts can also be approached on an exploratory basis with the aid of tuned percussion instruments. Thus the number of chime bars required to play a familiar phrase can be discovered aurally, as can scale structures and the need for chromatic alterations. Playing by ear familiar melodies and phrases patterned by the teacher is another valuable form of aural discovery. It involves both tonal memory and inner hearing, demands intense concentration, affords a useful preparation for improvisatory work and is an enjoyable and stimulating form of aural training. Exploratory methods can also be used to introduce harmonic concepts. For this purpose, use can be made of one of the many familiar songs and rounds which admit of a tonic and dominant accompaniment. After the song has been accompanied throughout by tonic harmony, the need for dominant harmonies at certain points will be determined aurally, and later from notation; the initial procedure will involve aural trial and error and notation will be used for purposes of reinforcement and explanation.

There can be no doubt that concepts, insights, knowledge, skills and positive attitudes are most effectively developed in a free, flexible and stimulating environment which encourages individual initiative, self-discovery and judgment; the music corners to be found in many classrooms in infant schools are an indication of the importance attached to first-hand exploratory experiences. This emphasis on learning by doing, so persuasively advocated by John Dewey,[3] has invigorated and indeed transformed primary education. It has also produced revolutionary changes in the roles of both teachers and their pupils. The teacher is no longer the autocratic centre of attention, disseminating information and knowledge and relying upon drill and rote learning for the assimilation of 'inert facts'. The function of the teacher now is thus not simply to transmit and impart. Neither is the pupil regarded merely as a passive receiving organism, a shape to be moulded or a receptacle to be filled. The once-popular action song and the percussion band, with its automaton-like players and its even more automaton-like child conductor, are relics of an age which preferred filling in to drawing out and ignored the importance of inventiveness and imagination.

Reaction against rigid formality and over-directed teaching, with its reliance on external discipline, should not however lead us to underestimate the importance of the role of the teacher in organizing and controlling musical experiences and learning situations in which concepts can be systematically acquired and applied. Activities and experiences must be purposeful if they are to be guided into constructive, educative channels of response. Thus the successful teacher of music and movement, while avoiding having recourse to prescribed, stereotyped response patterns, will acknowledge the need to give the pupils guidance in building up a basic vocabulary of movement. In creative work also, learning by discovery does not preclude directional guidance of any sort. Music is a coherent and disciplined art form: licence has no place in it, for freedom and discipline are inseparably linked. Creative work involves sensitive and sympathetic guidance rather than imposed, formal instruction and questions of technique should be introduced as aids to coherent and articulate expression, not as inhibiting restrictions; on the other hand, the argument that any degree of control on the part of the teacher or suggested improvements will have a deleterious effect on the freedom, spontaneity and freshness of children's expressional work is pretentious humbug which encourages quite erroneous ideas about the artistic creative processes. The creation of a conceptual framework thus involves guided musical growth and a stimulating and flexible, but organized environment.

Conceptual growth depends upon the provision of a varied range of experiences of a concrete nature in which children can explore and manipulate the raw materials of music; hence the value of pitch games, simple instrumental playing and movement as preliminary aids to the growth of aural perception and the understanding of notational abstractions. According to Piaget,[4] the principal stages in intellectual development are the sensory-motor (from birth to two years), pre-conceptual intelligence (two to four), intuitive thinking (four to seven), during which period the learner is handicapped by various perceptual problems and lacks conservation, concrete operations (eight to eleven), when he is still dependent on a concrete framework, and formal operations (eleven to fourteen or fifteen), when he can begin to think propositionally and reason without dependence on concrete situations. Although attempts have been made to apply Piaget's theory of conservation to musical development,[5] little attention has so far been given to the applicability of his theory of concept formation to the building of a framework of musical concepts or to the relevance to musical growth of his description of the developmental stages in intellectual growth. It is clear, however, that until the child reaches the age of eleven his musical experiences must be of an essentially concrete nature. This raises many problems because of music's intangibility and dynamic character and necessitates a consideration of the role of analogies, imagery and symbols in music education and of the question of tonal memory.

ANALOGIES

Since music exists only in time, it is difficult to discuss music without having to borrow such terms as 'form', 'colour', 'texture' and 'phrase' from other art forms. John Locke warned that 'similes always fail in some part',[6] but, providing we are careful not to press them too far, analogies can clarify the meaning of somewhat abstract musical concepts.

Perhaps the most obvious analogy is that between music and language. Herbert Spencer, in 'The Origin and Function of Music', asserted that music arose from a deliberate attempt to reproduce the inflections of speech. Music, like language, is a two-way means of communication, having a dynamic, evolving syntax and grammar. There are several structural parallels: balancing, antithetical phrases can form the basis of patterning between teacher and pupil and the rhythms of verbal question and answer phrases can be used as a starting point in creative work. It is also possible to explain cadences in terms of musical punctuation and to develop concepts of pulse and pulse groupings by making use of the metrical two-ness and three-ness which is common to both music and poetry. The close association between music and speech is responsible for the influence exerted by speech patterns and inflections on the traditional music of various countries. Thus there is an obvious connection between the characteristic rhythmic patterns of Hungarian folk melody and the practice of stressing first syllables in the Hungarian language.

Language has an extremely important symbolizing function in enabling us to analyse and classify concepts. Because of music's linguistic characteristics, the teacher of music can benefit from the considerable amount of research which has been conducted into the nature and acquisition of language and reading skills. The methods of such men as Yorke Trotter[7] and Suzuki are based on the assumption that the processes involved in learning the language of music should correspond closely to those involved in learning one's mother tongue. The basis of learning in both cases is imitation, and linguistic facility emerges from use and experience of language. Words can conceal lack of true understanding and empty verbalism results from their being treated as substitutes instead of vehicles for concepts; the same can apply to notational symbols when they are divorced from their associated aural concepts.

Differing views are held about the value of the paradigms known as French rhythm names. Some teachers feel that they are too childish for use with children in secondary schools, are an unnecessary additional body of terms to be learnt and are confusing when more complex rhythmic patterns are introduced. There is much to be said therefore for the use of familiar English speech patterns to develop rhythmic concepts. The names of familiar objects, places and people can be used to introduce rhythm cells as unified complexes of sound. These can be translated into percussive sounds and used for patterning and recognition; they can also be treated as building blocks by being joined together to form more extended patterns, and dictation can take the form of noting down the sequence of rhythmic cells employed by the teacher in tapping or playing a phrase. An awareness of the contrasting effect of a number of cells, based on words linked to the same topic, can be developed by their being used simultaneously, ostinato-style: thus over a steady pulse or simple bass ostinato, each performer can enter at regular intervals with his own rhythmic pattern. In addition to cumulative ostinato exercises, ostinati can be used to accompany instrumental pieces, choral speech and songs.

The use in choral speech of the words of familiar songs and singing games, nursery, number and humorous nonsense rhymes, proverbs and other jingles can have a beneficial effect on enunciation and rhythmic buoyancy in singing. Choral speech, highlighted by percussion accompaniment, can be developed by a combination of rhythmic speech, tapped rhythmic patterns and ostinati derived from one or two words of the verse. Just as the contrasting effects of different rhythm cells were explored by combining them in ostinato exercises, so should more extended rhythmic patterns be combined. Thus the rhythm of a proverb or jingle can be tapped canonically or in diminution or augmentation, or the rhythms of two such proverbs or jingles can be tapped simultaneously. At first such exercises will be performed by two separate groups of children; with increasing experience, some children may be able to carry out individually such simultaneous operations. Before leaving the subject of speech rhythms, it must be emphasized that it is generally possible to fit more than one rhythmic pattern to a group of words, whilst preserving the natural verbal accentuation. Instead of being pushed into rhythmic strait-jackets, words should be studied from the point of view of their various rhythmic possibilities; compound time should be frequently used and the less familiar time signatures explored.

In addition to these linguistic connections, there are also parallels between the literature of music and that of prose. Indeed no study of the music of the nineteenth-century romantic composers would be complete without some consideration of such literary influences as those of Jean Paul Richter on Schumann and E. T. A. Hoffmann on Weber; Liszt, Mendelssohn and Berlioz were keenly interested in the work of contemporary poets and dramatists and were themselves accomplished writers.

The part played by visual imagery and chromaesthesia (coloured hearing) in listening to music may be responsible for the number of parallels which have been drawn between music and painting. In his *Essay on Musical Expression*, first published in 1752, Charles Avison included a chapter dealing with the analogies between the two arts. This chapter, modelled to some extent on Dryden's 'Parallel between Poetry and Painting' (1695), reveals the influence of the doctrine of the affections: Freneuse had written of the 'bond of union' between the arts, 'which makes what can be said of each of them almost common to all'.[8] Avison explained that he was using the parallel between music and painting because the latter was 'an art more obvious in its principles'. He was writing of course for a new reading public. The middle class society, which had emerged as a political and economic power in the previous century, by now exerted a considerable influence on English cultural life. During the present century, the work of several painters has had a significant effect on musical styles. Obvious examples are the influence of Manet on Debussy, Picasso on Stravinsky and Kandinsky on Schoenberg.

Analogies can be used to clarify ideas, to draw attention to the close connection and interaction between the arts and to provide a basis for subject correlation. They can also be a means of developing stylistic awareness and an understanding of the artistic and social backgrounds against which composers have worked. Although it may be claimed that the greatest works of art transcend both time and space, they nonetheless reflect the spirit of the age in which they are created and are expressions of their own periods and cultures. It is therefore valuable to have some understanding of general cultural and environmental influences, as well as of the musical conventions, vocabularies, idioms, forms and styles of the periods in which composers have lived. Only in this way can stylistic confusion be avoided and historical listening developed. Thus, as Bukofzer has pointed out, if baroque music is to be fully appreciated, it is necessary for the listener to realize that 'display of splendour was one of the main social functions of music for the counter-reformation and the baroque courts, made possible only through money'.[9] Provided always that we bear in mind the limitations of analogies, useful stylistic parallels can be drawn between the early seventeenth-century homophonic style and the transition from Gothic to Renaissance architecture, and between the creative output of Reynolds, Pope and Mozart, Constable, Thomson and Beethoven, Turner, Wordsworth and Schumann.

IMAGERY

The process of perception is one of the most vital

elements in concept formation for conceptual levels of attainment are essentially dependent on perceptual levels. Perceptual awareness is developed by exercising the whole range of sensory apparatus and it is important in music education to appeal to the visual, tactile and kinaesthetic senses in order to clarify and reinforce auditory impressions. These sensory-perceptual experiences have to be organized, generalized and systematized if a secure conceptual framework is to be built.

Motor imagery plays an important part in the response to music because of the interconnected psychological and physiological effects of music and the resulting close association between musical and bodily rhythms. Regular periodicity is a fundamental characteristic of both physiological processes and musical rhythms. From an early age children enjoy responding to the rhythm of music with bodily movement. The popularity of the see-saw, the rocking-horse, the swing and such activities as skipping and singing games can be attributed to the satisfaction and pleasure instinctively derived from rhythmic muscular motion (usually of a two-fold or duple nature). Work-songs, pulling-shanties and marches illustrate the fact that certain repetitive tasks can be performed more easily and with greater enjoyment if carried out to a regular movement, accompanied by music. People of all ages tend to listen to music with their feet and dance music of all types, as well as 'pop' music, with its convulsive, relentless beat, to which the young seem unable to resist responding physically, are manifestations of the pulsating life of man and his natural environment.

Singing games, music and movement and dance all provide obvious opportunities for children to respond physically to music and to explore its rhythmic, structural and expressive qualities. Hand and arm movements can also be used to develop various rhythmic concepts. Finger snapping, 'hand-talking' (using finger tips, palms and cupped hands) and knee-slapping (*patschen*) can be used for such purposes as patterning, rhythmic questions and answers and speech and song accompaniments. By emphasizing the need for light, buoyant movements and encouraging the independent use of both hands, this type of activity can develop muscular co-ordination and form a valuable introduction to the playing of tuned and un-tuned percussion instruments. Other hand and arm movements which can be used as gesture symbols to develop motor imagery include hand staves, hand signs, arm signals, beating time, hand-swing movements and tracing melodic contours; rhythm shorthand also provides an opportunity to respond to music with con-tinuous, rhythmical hand movements.

Visual, spatial, kinaesthetic, tactile and auditory imag-ery are all involved in the playing of musical instruments. Instrumental playing can provide creative as well as interpretative experiences, interest those children to whom singing makes only a limited appeal and be an incentive to learning musical notation. Keyboard-type instruments, including xylophones and melodicas, are particularly valuable for exploring and developing such concepts as tonal direction, intervallic relationships, chords, scale structures and tonal organization. A glockenspiel, placed vertically at the side of a modulator or stave, can be a most useful audio-visual aid to the development of these pitch concepts.

The function of visual and motor imagery is to rein-force, not act as a substitute for, auditory imagery. There is a serious risk, if instrumental playing is approached in the wrong way, of associating notational symbols with muscular movements rather than aural images and this may be responsible for lack of facility later on in such skills as transposing, improvising and playing from memory. This tendency can be counteracted to some extent by singing melodies before playing them, singing one part while playing the other parts of a simple contrapuntal piece, playing familiar melodies by ear or recognizing them from their notation.

Because of the risk of undeveloped aural perception, great importance is attached to the place of solfège in the training of French instrumentalists. Kodály, unlike Orff, was opposed to an early introduction of instruments, since he believed that the inner ear develops satisfactorily only if initial pitch concepts are essentially vocal and not dependent upon visual or motor imagery. He attached great importance to unaccompanied singing, arguing that the best accompaniment to a voice was another voice, and emphasized that, when instrumental playing was introduced, the voice should not be neglected.

It was this approach to the formation of pitch concepts which led Kodály to recognize the distinctive values of the tonic sol-fa system. Although this system, with its hand signs, hand staves and modulators, makes some use of visual and motor imagery, it is essentially a vocal system of aural training. Curwen himself stressed that it should be regarded as an 'interpreting', not alternative, notation. With its aural mnemonics and mental effects, tonic sol-fa's relationship to staff notation may be compared with the relationship of i.t.a. or phonetic spelling to traditional orthography. The sol-fa syllables can be gradually introduced in association with commonly-occurring configurations in familiar songs to objectify tonal relationships. Kodály valued the tonic sol-fa system particularly as an aid to the beginner in finding his bearings on the stave and understanding the harmonic implications of melodies. In Hungarian musical education it remains a principal means of aural training long after fixed names and instrumental playing have been introduced. Various number systems, mostly derived from Rousseau's cipher notation, have been advocated. Although they are obviously useful in the development of intervallic and harmonic concepts, English numbers are much less attractively singable than sol-fa syllables and the arguments so far advanced in favour of the use of numbers have lacked real conviction.

Reference was made earlier to the risks involved in using motor imagery to develop auditory imagery. Similar risks are involved in the use of notational symbols. There are two reasons for this. Firstly, there is a tendency to introduce symbols before children have had adequate and varied aural experience; musical symbols should represent what is already aurally familiar to the children and should thus be used for purposes of consolidation rather than introduction. The other reason is that it is dangerously easy to divorce symbols from their associated sounds and the teacher must constantly reinforce the bond between symbol and sound. Provided the teacher is aware of these problems, he can use symbols to develop and refine aural concepts, since the eye is the principal channel of communication; symbols are a specialized form of conceptual thought and are an essential aid to the understanding and manipulation of concepts.

There are various types of symbol which can be used for musical conceptualization. Contours, modulators and picture notation can be used to develop pitch concepts and shorthand rhythm symbols can be employed in conjunction with sol-fa letters. Staff notation can be approached by means of one- and two-line staves or by buckwheat shape notation, which has been used with success in a number of American schools. The spacing of the vertical lines in 'Klavarskribo' notation and of the horizontal lines in 'Totten' notation is related to the pattern of the black keys of the piano keyboard. Reference was made in the previous chapter to the use of graphic outline scores by certain contemporary composers; coloured graphic scoring is also used in the 'Tonescript' charts, films and film-strips of orchestral works.

The influence of colour imagery in music is evident in the use of such terms as 'tone colour', 'chromatic' and 'coloratura'. Musicians also frequently associate certain keys with certain colours. This close association of colours and sounds is known as chromaesthesia and is probably the commonest form of synaesthesia. Those who have attempted to explain this phenomenon have pointed out that both sound and light are vibratory stimuli and they have compared the seven notes in the diatonic scale with the seven colour-bands in the spectrum. The sound–colour association has greatly interested several composers: colour organs have been made, Scriabin used a light keyboard and Bliss composed a 'Colour' Symphony. More attention could be given to the use of colour in teaching music-reading skills. It has been reported that colour story reading has achieved better results than the initial teaching alphabet. In addition to conveying additional phonetic information, colours have provided greater motivation because of their superior aesthetic appeal over black and white. Coloured music symbols have been used in conjunction with the Hohner 'Clarina'; they are a principal feature of the Hubicki 'Colour Staff'[10] and the present writer has made use of five coloured shape notes in connection with the teaching of pentatonic music.

MEMORY

Investigations into the nature of musical ability all confirm that tonal memory is one of the most significant factors in musical ability and is a basic requirement for all musical activities, whether they involve creativity, performance or listening. Absolute pitch is a form of retentive memory for pitch, or perhaps simply for a particular note or group of notes; it is an ability which can be developed through practice and experience. Patterning is one of the many procedures adopted in class lessons which can improve tonal memory skills. Imitative tapping of the teacher's patterns by individuals and groups can involve memorizing not only the rhythm but also the dynamic level, tempo and type of tapping adopted; alternatively, members of the class may be asked to respond with contrasting dynamics. The children may progress to patterning one another's phrases round the class, the teacher tapping the pulse to maintain a steady tempo and continuity between phrases. Similar procedures can be adopted for melodic echoing and sequential patterning.

Rhythmic and pentatonic canons, in which patterns and repetitions overlap, are a natural extension of patterning activities. A rhythmic canon may take the form of repeating the teacher's improvised pattern at one or two bars' distance or of the class being divided into two groups to tap canonically a rhythmic pattern written on the blackboard. The use of instruments of contrasting pitch or timbre can be helpful. Some children may be able to tap the rhythms of familiar melodies canonically, using one hand on each knee. Alternatively they may be able to sing a familiar melody and tap its rhythm canonically, perhaps even in diminution or augmentation. Improvised melodic canons should initially be restricted to some or all the notes of the pentatonic scale.

Learning songs by rote, identifying familiar songs, the rhythms of which are tapped by the teacher, and playing them by ear are additional methods of developing tonal memory skills. Tapping, singing and playing rhythmic and melodic patterns shown on flash cards are activities which demand great concentration. Also valuable for tonal memory purposes is dictation when it takes the form of writing familiar melodies from memory or unfamiliar melodies *after* they have been played. As a development of canonic work, some children may be able to sing a familiar melody while tapping the rhythm of another, or to tap the rhythms of two such melodies simultaneously, using one hand on each knee.

GROWTH PATTERNS

Reference has already been made to the need to make adequate provision for individual differences in musical ability, experience and interest. It is necessary also to take into account the influence of emotional, physical and social growth patterns on conceptual development. Thus the teacher's choice of music and musical activities must be appropriate to the pupils' stage of growth if it is to meet their emotional and social needs and interests. Muscular development and other physiological factors will similarly help to determine the teacher's approach to movement, instrumental playing, singing and music reading. The fact that the large arm and leg muscles are the first to develop and be controlled will result in emphasis being placed initially on fundamental movements; progress will gradually be made to differentiated and refined movements involving the use of the smaller muscles. In instrumental playing also, regard will be paid to the children's stage of muscular co-ordination and sensory discrimination. The first instruments to be introduced will involve principally the use of the larger arm muscles: the order of instrumental difficulty thus is probably untuned percussion instruments, tuned percussion, simple wind and stringed instruments, brass band instruments and finally orchestral instruments; physical factors will also determine the type of part the children are expected to play. In singing, physical growth patterns make it necessary to give careful attention to such factors as phrasing, vocal and dynamic range and complexity of vocal line, and these patterns must be taken into account in dealing with monotones and children whose voices are changing. In the case of music reading also, questions of physical maturation have an important bearing on such factors as the size and layout of the notation in the children's copies.

It is clear then that teaching for conceptual growth involves a skilful adjustment of content and method to maturation levels. However, although notational symbols should not be introduced prematurely, it is important not to adopt a rigid, inflexible attitude towards the subject of music reading readiness. Music reading is not an activity which is suddenly introduced for the first time when a child reaches the age of six, seven or eight. It is rather a gradual initiation, beginning with the introduction of gesture symbols, the pace depending on aptitude and experiential background. Neither is instrumental readiness the product simply of maturation; in the past overcautious views have resulted in children of primary school age being deprived of opportunities to acquire certain instrumental skills.

Learning is an organic, developmental process and teaching must be based on the principles of sequential growth. Little research has been conducted so far into the application of developmental psychology to musical education. It is clear, however, that a knowledge of the principles of Gestalt psychology can be of considerable value to the teacher of music. Gestalt psychologists argue that learning is a gradual process of differentiation, in which the whole, at first vaguely apprehended, becomes progressively articulated and clarified as the learner gains understanding of the constituent elements. Behaviour is thus changed by reshaping total patterns, rather than by piecing details together. It follows that it is necessary in teaching to proceed from the whole to the part, the general to the specific, the known to the unknown, the concrete to the abstract, the sound to the symbol and the simple to the complex. In creative work, children become increasingly aware of the rhythmic and melodic details of their improvisations and capable of analysing the procedures involved. In learning songs, since the mind does not work by building up parts, it is important to begin by gaining a general impression of the song as a whole. The same applies to the study of musical form: although analysis can be valuable for clarifying inter-relationships, a pedantic preoccupation with dissection, syntax and formulae can prevent a listener or performer appreciating a work as a musically-intelligible whole and as a unified, growing organism. Insight into the total effect of large-scale instrumental forms can be gained from a study of songs which exemplify the forms on a miniature scale. In teaching music-reading skills also, it is important to remember that the mind functions by analysing wholes and to present notes, not in isolation, but in the context of musically-meaningful configurations.

Dynamic teaching has a sense of direction and purpose, it provides for continuous growth and the progressive, sequential development of concepts and skills. The teaching of music, especially in the fields of creativity and movement, too often lacks these characteristics. It tends to be static, insufficiently demanding and geared to what has been termed the yesterday of the child's development. Although conceptual growth involves the acquisition of additional concepts (concept attainment), it is not simply an additive process, but one of gradual reconstruction in which existing concepts are constantly modified, refined and enriched. Effective teaching has been likened to a continuous upward spiral:[11] concepts are not introduced once and for all, but are regularly reintroduced with increasing specificity, so that pupils can explore them in greater depth, apprehend them with increasing clarity and thus gain in aural perception.

Advances made in techniques of programmed learning have served to draw attention to the importance of individualized learning procedures based on the need for feedback, immediate and regular reinforcement of correct responses and the presentation of material in an organized and continuous sequential pattern. Little systematic research has been conducted into the most effective ways of selecting and presenting musical material in a developmental sequence. Musical ability investigations[12] have thrown some light on to the sequential development of musical concepts. They have indicated, for instance, that rhythmic concepts develop before pitch concepts and pitch concepts before harmonic concepts; we also know that rhythmic and pitch perception are virtually independent of one another. With regard to the hierarchical nature of pitch concepts, it is reasonable to assume that intervallic concepts cannot be realized until directional concepts have been mastered. Similarly harmonic concepts of vertical organization are probably developed most effectively from those of linear organization. Thus, although rhythmic and pitch concepts can, to some extent, be developed independently, the majority of concepts are essentially inter-related: as mentioned earlier, the elements of music combine to produce expressive effects.

It is possible to apply the recapitulation theory of educational development to musical education as a guide to the sequencing of subject matter. This theory is based on the assumption that the stages in the individual's musical growth correspond to those in the growth of music itself. Thus, for example, a sequential treatment of musical notation would take account of the fact that early notational devices have included the use of colour and staves of fewer than five lines. *Orff-Schulwerk* is influenced to some extent by this theory: hence the early use of pentatonic material, borduns and modes, and the delay in introducing the sub-dominant and dominant chords, because of the inhibiting effect of premature conformity to more recent harmonic idioms.

Lack of precise knowledge about the hierarchical structure of musical concepts makes it impossible at present to break down musical materials into suitably small sequential steps and is responsible for conflicting views on such topics as the most effective sequence of tonal configurations and keys and the relative value of various notational devices. A logical sequence is not necessarily a psychologically-appropriate sequence. For instance, it may be logical to deal with simple time before compound. This, however, fails to take account of the quite different psychological effects of a Beethoven Scherzo, in fast simple triple time, and a Chopin Nocturne, in slow compound duple. Until such problems are solved, it will not be possible to build secure or elaborate conceptual frameworks in music.

CONTINUITY IN MUSIC EDUCATION

The theme of this chapter has been the need to provide for continuous musical growth through the sequential development of concepts and skills and to regard musical education as a progressive, cumulative process. This process begins, of course, during the pre-school years, which represent the most crucial period of a child's development. During these early years, a child who is fortunate enough to be brought up in a stimulating musical environment will gain varied formative experiences which will help to establish positive attitudes towards music, lay the foundations of aural perception and raise his level of intellectual functioning. By having his attention drawn to the qualities and contrasts of the sounds of his environment, his interest in and receptivity to sound will develop; through listening to music and learning a number of nursery rhymes and finger play songs, he will find his singing voice and acquire some basic musical concepts.

The importance of pre-school musical development is recognized in the system of Shinichi Suzuki, President of the Talent Education Research Society of Japan. By emphasizing the importance of musical imitation and repetition, he seeks to provide a musical counterpart to children's early linguistic experience. He suggests that if a recorded piece of music is played every day in a baby's room, the baby will begin to listen attentively; from the age of five months, an additional piece is played daily. This forms the background to learning the violin at about the age of three. Notation is not introduced for some time, reliance being placed upon learning by ear; the record player thus continues to be an important aid to learning. Children are taught to play the violin in large numbers: indeed Suzuki has so far taught over 70,000 children.

Some of the most interesting developments in musical education have been carried out in our primary schools. The general practitioner system of teaching, though open to certain objections, has many virtues. The teacher is able to introduce music naturally and spontaneously into class activities when the children are in a receptive mood and she can relate it to other subjects. Moreover the regular class teacher is more likely to secure a lively response from her pupils than one who, although perhaps a more skilful musician, does not know the pupils as well. The principal disadvantage of the system is the fact that so many primary school teachers lack confidence in their ability to teach music. Consequently the quality of primary school music is extremely variable and, since a secondary school may draw from ten or eleven primary schools and a comprehensive from over forty, there is generally a serious lack of continuity between music in primary and secondary schools. This state of affairs is aggravated by the uneven distribution of musically-competent teachers among primary schools and by the fact that only 4% of students in colleges of education choose to take the main course in music.

Many teachers who lack musical skill and confidence find broadcasts to schools very helpful. At present, sound broadcasts for primary schools include *Music Box* (for older infants), *Time and Tune* (for 7 to 8 year olds), *Music*

Workshop I (for 8 to 9 year olds), *Music Workshop II* (for 9 to 10 year olds) and *Singing Together* (for 9 to 12 year olds); there are also two series of music and movement programmes, for 5 to 6 and 6 to 8 year olds respectively, and *Music, Movement and Mime* for 9 to 11 year olds. Television programmes for primary schools include *Making Music*, a programme intended for 10 to 11 year olds.

There is an increasing availability of music courses for teachers in primary schools. These may take the form of residential summer schools or regular meetings held at music centres. Music workshops are also providing a valuable service. Teachers who lack confidence in their musical ability would probably welcome guidance from visiting music specialists, who would do some teaching in three or four primary schools in addition to offering advice to members of staff. In Belfast, a number of music specialists have been appointed to visit the authority's primary schools in an advisory capacity and for some time in America, the practice has been to appoint a music consultant to work in three elementary schools, thus serving about thirty-six teachers. Continuity and co-ordination could also be improved if music specialists in secondary schools took a closer interest in the musical activities of their contributory primary schools. These are, of course, only make-shift remedies and the only really satisfactory solution is to provide improved musical facilities for intending primary school teachers while they are still at school and college. Special music courses could be provided for sixth-formers who hope to go on to colleges of education, and in the colleges themselves it has become increasingly recognized that non-specialist, basic music courses must be provided for all intending primary school teachers. Emphasis in such courses is placed upon increasing the confidence of the students by concentrating upon the type of practical music-making skills which will be of greatest value in the classroom situation and by acquainting them with a wide range of suitable teaching material. In the case of those students whose musical development has been seriously neglected, the most effective remedial methods are likely to be derived from the creative music-making techniques currently being practised in primary schools.

In this discussion of continuous musical growth, reference has been made to the importance of the pre-school years and the need for a greater degree of continuity between primary and secondary school music. Further interruptions to musical growth take place in those secondary schools which fail to provide continuous, progressive and systematic courses in music. Music societies and other out-of-class voluntary activities are inadequate substitutes for such courses. A difficult, but most important, responsibility of the teacher of music in a secondary school is to ensure, as far as possible, that his pupils' musical growth does not cease when they leave school. Indeed it may be claimed that the success and effectiveness of a music teacher's work must be judged ultimately by the attitudes his pupils will adopt towards music in adulthood and by their future musical interests. It is true that, since childhood has its own meaning and value, music in schools must satisfy children's present needs. At the same time, children must be provided with the skills and insights necessary for continued independent musical growth and development, and a varied range of musical experiences which may form the basis of enduring recreational interests and thus enrich both the present and the future.

NOTES TO CHAPTER 4

1 Brocklehurst, J. B., *Pentatonic Song Book*, Schott, 1968.
2 Schafer, R. M., *The Composer in the Classroom*, B.M.I. Canada, Ltd, 1965; *Ear Cleaning*, B.M.I. Canada, Ltd, 1967.
3 Dewey, J., *Experience and Education*, New York: Macmillan, 1938.
4 Beard, R. M., *An Outline of Piaget's Developmental Psychology for Students and Teachers*, Routledge & Kegan Paul, 1969.
5 Pflederer, M., 'Conservation Laws applied to the Development of Musical Intelligence', *Journal of Research in Music Education*, xv (1967), 3.
6 Locke, J., *Conduct of the Understanding*, 1690, Sect. xxxii.
7 Yorke Trotter, T. H., *Music and Mind*, Methuen, 1924.
8 Strunk, O., *Source Readings in Music History*, Faber, 1950.
9 Bukofzer, M. F., *Music in the Baroque Era*, Dent, 1947.
10 Chapple, B., 'Colour Staff', *Music Teacher*, xlviii (1969), Nos. 6 (June) & 7 (July).
11 Bruner, J. S., *The Process of Education*, New York: Vintage Books, 1963.
12 Bentley, A., *Musical Ability in Children and its Measurement*, Harrap, 1966.

5

SKILLS

MUSIC AS COMMUNICATION

Many of the educative values attributed to music, and especially those concerned with music's functional role in child development, are based on the assumption that music is a means of non-verbal communication. The purpose of this chapter is to examine the principal links in the chain of musical communication and to consider the extent to which teachers of music can strengthen such links by developing creative, literacy, performance, movement and listening skills.

The first in the series of links relating to musical composition involves the various artistic, social and environmental factors which influence the thought-processes and emotions expressed in the music, as well as any literary, liturgical, pictorial or choreographic stimuli to creativity. Whatever is written about the workings of the creative imagination is inevitably conjectural since the source of all artistic creativity is the unconscious mind. Although some attempts have been made at carrying out psychological structural analyses of the processes involved in musical creativity, music is likely to remain 'a symbolic language of the unconscious mind whose symbolism we shall never be able to fathom'.[1] Moreover, little is to be accomplished by attempting to draw a dividing line between creative imagination and technique. Indeed, in the case of a composer such as Schubert, the two aspects are virtually inseparable.

The next series of links relates to the performance of music. Because of the limitations inherent in our system of musical notation in its present stage of evolution and of the latitude which must exist in any artistic activity, there can be no one 'correct' interpretation of a musical work. Nonetheless, in spite of the considerable re-creative element in interpretation, the performer must pay scrupulous regard to the composer's intentions if these links in the chain of communication are not to be impaired. The performer is particularly handicapped in this respect in performing the music of the seventeenth and eighteenth centuries. Because of the considerable improvisatory element in the music of the time (as in jazz today), the scores incorporate such devices as ornaments and figured bass lines and are often guides to the performer rather than precise blueprints. Thus if he is to play an Italian Adagio of the late seventeenth century in an authentic manner, a performer must be able to interpret the musical score in accordance with the musical conventions of the time. He will take account of recent musicological research and view certain nineteenth-century editorial accretions with suspicion. At the same time he will recognize the fact that absolute authenticity is impossible and avoid making a fetish of *Aufführungspraxis*.

The final series of links in the chain of musical communication involves the response of the listener. As indicated earlier, the nervous system forms the basis of the listener's emotional reaction and, since the immediate response to auditory stimuli is a physical one, sounds are, as it were, felt before being intellectually apprehended.

The number of links in the chain of communication is variable. Thus the chain can be shortened if the performer is singing or playing for himself alone or if the composer is also the performer. It is for this reason that recordings made by such composer–performers as Rachmaninoff are generally regarded as definitive interpretations. Links can also be added to the chain, with the consequent danger of impairing the composer–listener communication. Thus the authenticity of the edition the performer is using, the quality of the musical instrument he is playing, the fidelity of the electronic reproduction and the acoustics of the room in which the music is heard are all of great importance. The role of the engineer in broadcasting and recording is a vital one. He cannot compensate for poor creative ideas, of course, but can, for instance in recording 'pop' music, enhance and flatter the original sound.

The principal links in the chain of musical communication and their associated skills can be represented as follows:

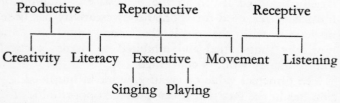

Literacy skills are needed by a composer in order to record his ideas and by a performer in order to interpret the composer's intentions; physical response involves both receptive and interpretative elements. Since receptivity is determined by the listener's insight into creative

99

and interpretative processes, skill in listening is influenced by the degree of skill possessed in the other five areas.

Creative skills will be considered first of all.

Much has been written in recent years about the need to awaken and develop children's creative powers and remarkable results have been achieved in language, art, movement and drama as a result of providing varied outlets for latent artistic creativity. In spite of the valuable pioneer work of Walford Davies and Yorke Trotter in Great Britain and of Mrs Satis Coleman[2] in the United States, the musical experiences provided in schools have, until recently, been mainly of a re-creative, interpretative nature. The remarkably natural musical inventiveness of young children has generally been underrated and neglected, and the apparent decline in the quality of their expressional work as they grow older may be attributed in part to the failure to provide them with varied opportunities for creative self-expression (for creative impulses are stifled by neglect) or to recognize that creativity is largely intuitive. Even in the professional training of musicians, the need for spontaneous creativity has been neglected, with the result that many musicians are musically tongue-tied and inhibited as far as practical improvisatory work is concerned.

The principal value of creative work in music education lies in the fact that it can provide opportunities for artistic self-expression, particularly for the less able child who does not wish to be reminded of his verbal inadequacies; all children have an instinctive desire for creative self-expression, and their first creative experiences can be developed from those spontaneous musical activities which form such a natural means of expression in early childhood. Such activities can be so organized that they bring together a wide range of interests and abilities and enable each child to contribute at his own level and develop musically at his own pace. A creative approach to music-making provides the most natural setting for exploring and experimenting with the basic raw materials of music and can have a vitalizing effect on the process of conceptual growth. For instance, devising song accompaniments can assist in the development of concepts of timbre, form, harmony and style. Creative work can develop auditory imagery and imagination and provide some insight into the creative processes of composition: thus, as was pointed out in Chapter 3, group improvisatory activities can be used as a means of introducing children to contemporary musical idioms. Creative work can also influence the development of musical judgment, taste and discrimination and stimulate creative activity in other subjects.

The problems facing the music teacher of guiding children's creative energies into controlled and disciplined expressive channels are different from, and perhaps more complex than, those facing teachers of other subjects. Music's intangibility, the nature of musical creativity and the need for notational and executive skills and tonal memory are but a few of the alleged stumbling blocks. A problem already referred to in the previous chapter concerns the importance of growth and development in creative work. In likening *Orff-Schulwerk* to a wild flower, Orff has emphasized the need for constant growth. As many teachers have discovered, *Orff-Schulwerk* is comparatively easy to introduce, but it requires a considerable degree of musical sophistication on the part of the teacher if continuous development is to be achieved and spontaneity maintained. The preservation of children's creative output also poses problems. In the early stages, the teacher may notate individual pupils' melodies, suggest improvements and sing or play the melodies, perhaps with harmonic support, or incorporate them into an instrumental piece. Children can also notate their own melodies, using flannelgraph staves or such symbols as sol-fa letters and shorthand signs; use can be made also of tuned percussion instruments, the bars of which are stamped with their letter names. The desirability of being able to record one's musical ideas on paper provides a valuable incentive to acquire literacy skills; for this reason, a selection of the children's compositions, written in class or at home, should be displayed on a notice-board or preserved in a folio. In the case of group improvisations, a tape recorder is a particularly valuable aid.

In considering the range of creative activities, it is important not to overlook the creative element in vocal and instrumental performance, movement and dance. The making of musical instruments is also an important creative activity: it is an interesting subject which can develop positive, creative attitudes towards music and provide incentives to acquire executive and literacy skills; it involves experimentation with sound-producing materials and sensitivity to intonation, sound quality and timbre and is thus a valuable form of aural training; it can develop an interest in elementary acoustics and the history and construction of musical instruments; most of the instruments which can be made in the classroom or workshop do not require costly materials, they involve simple performance skills, extend the range of possible ensemble activities and afford an introduction to the playing of more conventional instruments. In spite of these many advantages, excessive class time should not be devoted to instrument making and the importance of pleasing sound quality and accurate intonation should always be borne in mind.

Drums can be made in different pitches from small barrels and paint tins from which the tops and bottoms have been removed. Linen, calico and canvas, treated with dope, can be used for the heads, as can vellum and rubber inner tubing; in the case of the latter material, a double-headed drum can be made by lacing the two heads together. Pairs of maracas can be made from such plastic objects as egg-cups (taped together) and wool-winders as well as cardboard and wooden containers, coconut shells and bamboo lengths, corked at the opposite end to the node; various materials, such as rice, sand and lead shot, can be used to provide contrasting sounds, but the quality of sound will suffer if too much 'filling' is used. Different lengths of bamboo (one end closed) or half-inch dowel rod make suitable claves or rhythm sticks. A length of bamboo, with a node at each end and ridges filed across, makes an excellent guiro or rasp; its resonance is considerably improved if a slit is made along almost its whole length. A kitchen grater can also be used as a guiro. Other percussive effects can be achieved with sand blocks, coconut halves clapped together and Chinese blocks (wooden bricks of different pitches) struck with beaters.

Wine glasses and tumblers, tuned with water, and suspended cups, flower pots and bottles can be used to form pentatonic and diatonic scales. The oak or pine bars of xylophones and marimbas can be suspended or cushioned on foam plastic and mounted on wooden frames; aluminium alloy strips and copper rods are suitable materials for making glockenspiels and tubular bells. The making of bamboo pipes in schools dates back to 1932, when Margaret James founded the English Pipers' Guild: children can add holes to pre-voiced pipes of various sizes and decorate the instruments. The fingering for the first octave of the treble and tenor pipes is identical with that of the descant and treble recorders. The instrument is light-weight and its tone has a softer quality than that of the recorder. Simple one-string guitars and tea-chest basses can be made from reinforced boxes fitted with fingerboards; other simple stringed instruments have been developed from Egyptian prototypes. Their unstable tuning and quiet sound are, however, serious disadvantages in ensemble work. Mr Ronald Roberts[3] has done much to popularize the making of such stringed instruments as zithers, simple and bowed psalteries, Nordic lyres (fifteen strings, forming the scale of D major and plucked by finger or plectrum) and chordal dulcimers (four sets of strings, forming I, ii, IV and V chords and played with a felt-covered beater).

The most obvious of the methods which can be used to stimulate and develop musical inventiveness is based upon question and answer principles. Initial oral attempts may be based on the rhythms of verbal questions and answers. After they have gained some practice, members of the class may pose rhythmic questions. This may lead to a series of questions and answers, in which rhythmic continuity is maintained; such procedures may be used as interludes between verses or repetitions of songs to create ternary and rondo structures. With pupils' increasing experience, the questions should become longer, the answers being of varying lengths and use being made of less usual time signatures. Melodic questions and answers may initially be restricted to the use of two or three notes before progressing to the full pentatonic and diatonic scales. At the same time, practice should be given in evolving rhythms from speech patterns, applying rhythms to words and melodies to rhythms. Rhythmic and melodic treatments of familiar jingles, organized on a group basis and incorporating ostinati and question and answer interludes, can lead to the composing of new melodies for familiar nursery rhymes, jingles, songs and hymns.

The whole class should be involved in early attempts at setting unfamiliar words, attention being directed to the need to match the mood and expressiveness of the words; members of the class should be encouraged to suggest different rhythmic possibilities which preserve the natural verbal accentuation, to consider a suitable time signature and tempo, to decide whether the melodic line should be smooth or angular and whether a major or minor key would be more appropriate, to select a suitable form (bearing in mind the expressive functions of repetition and contrast) and decide upon the point or points of climax. After the melody has been composed, phrase by phrase, dynamic indications can be added. This type of approach to word setting can develop a feeling for words, interpretative sensitivity, musical concepts and aesthetic sensibility. Some children may be able to write both the words and melody, for instance, of a calypso and to compose simple rounds and descants as well as music for two voices or instruments.

Group improvisatory work may take several forms. Rhythmic and melodic ostinato exercises can be artistically satisfying; the teacher's function may be to maintain a steady pulse, supply a drone accompaniment or add a free improvised melodic strand to the texture. Other group compositions include rhythmic and melodic rondos and canons, improvisations within pre-arranged harmonic frameworks (including those used in familiar songs) and variations on familiar melodies. Melodies composed by members of the class can form a basis for group treatment: the use of repetition, variation and interludes can be considered in order to extend such melodies into longer pieces of music and instrumental accompaniments can be devised.

Interest is most likely to be maintained and developed if the various types of stimuli to musical creativity are fully explored. Such stimuli include movement, dance, mime, words, stories and plays as well as the instruments the children play. Kinaesthetic imagery plays an important part in creative work, and composing in such a form as *aaba* and with particular instruments in mind develops formal and stylistic concepts. Music is frequently used to stimulate creativity in movement and the reverse process is involved when children, inspired by motor imagery, improvise or write simple rhythms or melodies in particular dance styles. The creation of sound effects, melodies and *Leitmotive* to heighten the atmosphere of stories and plays and characterize the personalities involved provides a useful opportunity to develop an awareness of the expressive function of the constituent elements of music. The various creative activities which have been referred to can be brought together and integrated into a class project, such as the composition and performance of a small cantata or opera.[4]

LITERACY SKILLS

The importance of *musical literacy skills* is referred to in the Plowden Report;[5] considerable importance is also attached to literacy in the music examination for the C.S.E.[6] Music exists only in time and is the least tangible of the art forms; musical literacy can provide a key to musical understanding, aid the formation of aural concepts and develop auditory imagery and awareness, observation, concentration and memory. The musically-literate person is not dependent upon rote learning: literacy promotes self-reliance, it makes possible experimentation with the basic materials of music and independent exploration of its literature and is necessary in part-singing and instrumental playing.

Complaints about the poor standards of musical literacy in our schools are frequently expressed at conferences and in reports and journals. On the other hand, several arguments have been advanced by those who appear to be complacent about these poor standards. They assert that only a small proportion of children possess the necessary innate ability to achieve musical literacy because of the complexities of the language and notation of music; they draw attention to the limited amount of time available to develop other important musical skills and argue that energies can more profitably be devoted to actual music-making activities. These apologists also point out that songs can be taught by rote, that notational skills are irrelevant to enjoyment and aesthetic sensibility and that sight singing drudgery can all too easily result in boredom and a general distaste for music. Many of these arguments are of doubtful validity, for they are based upon serious misconceptions about the nature of musical ability, and it is therefore necessary to explore further the reasons for the disturbingly low standards of musical literacy in schools. There can be little doubt that such standards can be attributed in part to the variable quality of musical education in our primary schools: indeed the Plowden Report refers to 'the musical illiteracy of the great majority of teachers' in these schools. The situation is aggravated, moreover, by a lack of understanding on the part of many teachers about the nature and purpose of musical literacy and its relationship to the total musical curriculum and by the conflicting views of musical educationists about the suitability and effectiveness of various methods of approach. Even many of the teachers who conscientiously make provision for regular practice in class sight singing are disheartened by the absence of permanent, tangible results.

This reference to class sight singing provides an important clue to the cause of the limited progress made by many children in acquiring musical literacy skills. In the author's opinion, the conventional class sight singing lesson is of but limited value in developing musical literacy. Since it is possible for most members of the class to follow the lead of the few fluent readers, music reading organized on a class basis can all too easily conceal individual weaknesses and give a misleading idea of the progress being made. Class reading prevents adequate provision being made for individual differences in ability and experience. In a class of nine year olds, there may well be a span in reading ability of five years or more. A frequent result is that the abler children are bored and the less able, bewildered. Musical literacy is an individual skill, requiring individual practice and assessment rather than mass methods of instruction. In view of the size of classes in primary schools, it is important that more attention be given to devising methods of individualized instruction which will enable each child to proceed at his own uninterrupted pace and which can be used to supplement class music-making activities.

What is musical literacy? The term implies much more than a mere knowledge of the 'rudiments' of music and the technicalities of its notation: a person deaf from birth could acquire this knowledge. Too often musical literacy is approached as a pseudo-mathematical study, in which theory and practice are separated and symbols are divorced from their associated sounds, and in which children are drilled in the performance of unattractive, specially-devised sight singing material. Musical literacy implies cultivated aural perception, gained through varied perceptual experiences and music-making activities, conceptual understanding, a sympathy of eye and ear, well-developed tonal memory and imagery and the ability to hear inwardly, as well as a functional knowledge of the symbols and terminology of music.

Singing at sight involves three processes: the recognition of a printed symbol, the silent conversion of that symbol into an auditory image and the vocalization of the image. Musical dictation and written composition involve the conversion of auditory images into written symbols. Thus, in both cases, the conversion of either symbol into image or image into symbol is involved. Symbol–image conversion is one of the principal musical literacy skills and it is therefore necessary to devote considerable attention to the establishment and reinforcement of symbol–image bonds. It is for this reason that reference was made above to the importance of tonal memory, imagery, inner hearing and eye–ear co-ordination. Tonal memory is a valuable aid since it enables the learner to recognize the notation of previously-encountered rhythmic patterns and tonal configurations and to recall their sound. The various types of imagery discussed in the previous chapter are also important aids to conversion: thus kinaesthetic sensations associated with keyboard fingering or 'laryngeal' thinking may be brought into play. Such terms as auditory imagery, which involves a sensory-like experience without physical stimulus, and inner hearing have to be used because our language lacks the aural equivalent of the verb 'visualize': perhaps 'auralize' would be a usefully succinct term to describe this most crucially important element in musical literacy. A musically literate person is one for whom the symbols of notation have an essentially aural significance: he has a hearing eye and a seeing ear. It is therefore essential for the teacher to develop the closest possible association between notational symbols and their sounds and to develop the twin skills involving the auralization of symbols and the visualization of sounds through concurrent training in the closely-allied and mutually helpful activities of reading, dictation and creative work.

In teaching children to read prose, as much importance is attached to the ability to read silently with understanding as to the ability to read aloud. The same abilities apply to music reading. It was suggested earlier that three processes are involved in sight singing. The third process, the vocalization of an auditory image, may be regarded as involving an additional executive skill and it must therefore be remembered that it is possible for the accuracy of a pupil's auditory images to be masked by his vocal inadequacies. Musically intelligent playing at sight should also involve an intermediate process of auralization but, as was pointed out in the previous chapter, there is a danger here of associating notational symbols almost exclusively with particular keys or finger movements, of substituting kinaesthetic and motor imagery for auditory imagery and thus of failing to develop important habits of mental listening. It is possible to overcome such problems by letting members of the class sing the notes of a melody they are reading, while at the same time fingering the appropriate notes on dummy keyboards or on such instruments as recorders and melodicas. Practice should also be given in the silent recognition, from notation, of familiar melodies; deliberate errors can be included occasionally to test the aural alertness of the pupils and their ability to locate discrepancies between symbols and imagined sounds.

Music reading can take many forms, depending on the number of symbols and devices the teacher chooses to make use of. The following may be undertaken on a class, group or individual basis: tapping, playing or saying rhythm names from conventional rhythm notation or shorthand; playing, or singing to sol-fa, letter names, numbers or neutral syllables from staff notation, hand signs, modulators, hand staves or keyboard diagrams; singing to rhythm names from sol-fa letters or numbers and rhythm notation or shorthand or from staff notation. Individual reading practice is involved in converting familiar melodies into staff notation and identifying them from sol-fa, letters or numbers and rhythm notation or shorthand: conversion exercises can assist in the transition from sol-fa to staff notation, use being made from the outset of several keys; and the omission of such features as bar lines, time signatures or rhythm notation can result in the exercises involving both reading and dictation skills. Familiar melodies can also be identified from hand signs, sol-fa or staff modulators, hand staves, keyboard diagrams or rhythm, number or staff notation; the melodies for identification can be indicated by individual pupils as well as the teacher.

Reading is only one aspect of the ability to handle the language of music and practice should also be given in image–symbol conversion. Musical dictation is an obvious method of doing this and it provides a useful means of assessing individual progress. Both dictation and written composition (auto-dictation) demand auditory imagistic ability, for there is a clear association between aural imagery and aural imagination. The only difference in the mental imagining involved is that one is reproductive and the other, constructive.

Musical dictation, like reading, can be approached in a number of ways. Thus, as the teacher or a member of the class sings or plays a phrase, pupils can respond by tracing its contour or using the hand signs or hand stave (perhaps with their eyes closed), repeating it to sol-fa syllables, numbers, rhythm or letter names, pointing the notes on a modulator or dummy keyboard or playing it by ear. The notes of familiar melodies can be indicated by hand signs or pointed on a modulator, hand stave or keyboard. The rhythms can be written of phrases from familiar melodies, the words of which are given or from which certain notes or bars are omitted. Familiar melodies can be written, of which the words, the opening, the rhythm or the pitch are given, or from which certain notes or bars are omitted. The dictation of unfamiliar rhythms can be introduced by giving the notation of the phrase or sentence with certain notes or bars omitted or by basing the dictated phrase on bar-units, written in conventional or shorthand notation on the blackboard. In the case of unfamiliar melodies, either the rhythm or the pitch can be given (or each in alternate bars), or the complete phrase or sentence can be given, with certain notes or bars omitted.

Reference has been made to the use of familiar material for purposes of recognition (symbol–image) and recording (image–symbol). Such material is valuable in developing literacy skills for a number of reasons: its use involves the application of known-to-unknown and sound-to-symbol principles and it provides an effective means of developing tonal memory and the ability to recall music silently (the words of familiar songs being a useful aid). The use of familiar material enables the learner to work in a meaningful musical context and it can promote concentration, develop confidence and, since curiosity and a sense of relevance are such powerful incentives to learning, provide an interesting framework in which to acquire literacy skills. Perhaps most important of all, the use of such material provides a means of individualized instruction and of assessing progress made in silent reading.

The process of acquiring musical literacy skills may be conveniently divided into four stages: rote, observation, rote-and-note and note. During the initial pre-reading stage, when songs are taught by rote, the aim is to provide a variety of musical experiences which will help to establish a basic musical vocabulary and conceptual framework. This is equivalent in importance to providing young children with a background of spoken language in order to give meaning and purpose to reading.

Carefully selected 'observation' songs can be used during the second stage in order to familiarize children with the general appearance of musical notation, to convince them, even at this early stage, of the value, purpose and relevance of music reading to music-making activities and to establish a pattern approach to music reading. The initial observations will be of a general nature (thus resembling score following as opposed to score reading) and, in accordance with the principle of spiral growth, will gradually increase in specificity and complexity. The observations will principally involve basic rhythmic, pitch and formal concepts. Thus children can be asked to discover from their copies how many different rhythmic patterns occur (these can be written on the blackboard), to notice even and uneven rhythmic patterns and to locate in their copies rhythmic patterns tapped by the teacher. Attention will also be directed to such melodic features as contour, tonal direction and scale-wise and chordal motives; sol-fa can be used, as when the teacher sings a melodic fragment for the children to identify from their copies (e.g. 'To which words do we sing "doh-re-me-soh-lah-soh"?'). Formal concepts can be developed by asking children to discover examples of rhythmic and melodic repetition, sequence, modification and contrast: the words of songs can be a useful aid, in view of the tendency for verbal and musical repetitions to coincide.

After children have gained experience in associating commonly-occurring rhythmic patterns and melodic configurations with the notational complexes representing them, they can progress to the rote-and-note stage, which involves a mixture of learning by rote and reading previously encountered motives, and finally to the note stage.

Emphasis has been placed above on the recognition of patterns and configurations because of the importance of establishing from the outset a pattern approach to music reading. Methods which begin by developing focal awareness of isolated notes fail to take account of the fact that such notes lack musical meaning. By presenting reading as a tedious, mechanical process of deciphering and decoding individual notes one at a time, such methods succeed only in establishing faulty reading habits and negative attitudes towards music. The pattern approach to music reading, on the other hand, recognizes the importance of figuration in perception and presents musical patterns and configurations as visual and auditory functional unities. This approach may thus be compared to the 'Look and Say' method of teaching reading, which is based upon word patterns. As children gain in experience, more analytical procedures may be adopted, attention being drawn to smaller rhythmic and melodic groupings and practice being given in recognizing differences between pairs of very similar configurations.

An important objective in teaching music reading is thus to increase the pupils' visual span, by developing their ability to group notes into larger perceptual units. Improved lay-out of print in observation songs would make it somewhat easier to achieve this objective. Although some editions of songs do devote a separate line to each phrase, note spacing is generally determined by word spacing. One of the virtues of sol-fa notation is its use of equidistant spacing of bar lines and proportionate arrangement of notes according to their durational values. More experimental work could also be carried out into the use of note groupings and colour to present particular configurations as visual unities. Some research has been conducted in the United States into the use of short exposures of patterns, by means of simple and mechanized flash cards (tachistoscopes), in order to improve visual span and it is likely that increasing use will be made of films, film-strips, tape recorders and electronic staves in the development of musical literacy skills.

EXECUTIVE SKILLS

Executive skills are associated with the central series of links in the chain of musical communication. It has frequently been argued that, since the post-school musical experiences of the majority of pupils will involve listening rather than performing, school music should be concerned with the education of intelligent listeners, rather than unintelligent performers. H. G. Wells referred to the importance for the average music-lover of having a 'quickened ear rather than a disciplined hand' and the Hadow Report[7] declared that the aim of musical education should be 'rather the cultivation of a taste than the acquirement of a proficiency'. The provision of executive experiences in schools has in fact a dual purpose. For those children with aptitude for, and interest in, musical performance it is a means of acquiring performance skills which may lay the foundations of a leisure-time interest or, in some cases, of a professional career; for other children, executive experiences are a means of gaining some insight into interpretative processes and of developing concepts of style and expression, judgment, taste and artistic sensibility. It is true that an unimaginative and insensitive approach to the technical problems involved in acquiring vocal or instrumental skills can all too easily blunt aesthetic responsiveness and encourage negative attitudes towards music. In the majority of cases, however, pleasurable executive experiences have a beneficial effect on musical responsiveness. Indeed the enjoyment and understanding of a concert-goer who has had experience of performing music may be compared with that of the sports spectator who has himself been an active sportsman.

Singing has occupied a central position in most systems of musical education and remains the core of the musical curriculum. It is the most natural and spontaneous form of musical self-expression and requires no expensive equipment or sophisticated musicianship on the part of the teacher to achieve artistically satisfying results. Reference was made in the opening chapter to the physical and social benefits to be derived from singing. It is an important means of gaining a first-hand acquaintance with a large part of our musical heritage and of creating a framework of musical concepts. Since it can also be easily associated with the other five principal musical skills, singing can serve an important integrating purpose. Indeed it has been suggested that, because of its many values, singing alone can form an adequate basis for a class music programme. This view, however, fails to take account of the need for variety of activity within a lesson, of the differences which exist in musical aptitude and interest and of the mutually-helpful nature of the various musical skills. Moreover, as was pointed out earlier, there is no evidence of transfer of effect from an enthusiasm for singing to an interest in instrumental music. It is therefore necessary to introduce instrumental playing to complement vocal experience, strengthen further the executive links in the chain of musical communication and achieve a well-balanced musical curriculum.

The increased attention given to instrumental playing in state schools in recent years may be attributed in part to the influence of British public schools and American high schools, the work of various musical organizations and the publicity of the principal instrument manufacturers, and it has been made possible by the increased funds which have been allocated to instrumental provision and by the availability of cheaper, mass-produced instruments. The introduction of instrumental playing into class lessons provides an additional means of self-expression (for a musical instrument can become an extension of a player's personality) and it extends the scope of active participation and involvement, especially for those adolescent boys to whom community singing makes a limited appeal; because of the different types of imagery involved and the opportunities it provides for individual experimentation, instrumental playing can contribute to concept formation; it is a means of exploring the literature of music and developing an interest in solo instrumental and orchestral music, which forms a major part of the serious music heard at concerts and on the radio; the many types of instrument available and their widely-varying technical demands cater admirably for the different types of musical aptitude and interest; instrumental provision increases the likelihood of locating latent ability and the creation of heterogeneous instrumental groups, which is always possible, however little advanced a school's instrumental programme may be, is an effective way of developing possible leisure-time pursuits and thus of ensuring continued interest in music.

Limitations of space preclude any detailed discussion here of methods of vocal and instrumental instruction. For this the reader's attention is directed to the author's *Music in Schools.*[8] Instead, consideration will be given to the use of musical instruments in the classroom for purposes of accompanying singing. Activities involving voices and instruments are proving popular for a number of reasons. They can help the teacher who lacks pianistic facility, and in any case a few simple tuned and untuned instruments can often provide a more effective and authentic type of accompaniment than the piano. Such activities can make more realistic provision for varied abilities and interests than the conventional class singing lesson, for they enable each child to contribute vocally or instrumentally on his own level of competence; by giving a new dimension to class vocal work, these activities can add to interest in singing and have a beneficial effect on its quality, in particular its rhythmic buoyancy. Many children are less inhibited about improvising instrumentally than vocally and they can find instruments a useful aid in learning to sing rounds, canons and part-

songs. Evolving instrumental accompaniments can contribute to the development of a number of concepts.
Thus deciding upon instrumentation to match repetitions
and contrasts involves formal concepts. Selecting instruments and accompanying styles appropriate to various
cultures and periods of time aids the development of
stylistic concepts: idiomatic syncopated percussive effects
can be explored in accompanying Spanish, Latin-Ameri-
can and Caribbean songs; rhythmic ostinati, each note of
which is allocated to a different instrument, can be used
to accompany songs from the Far East, and attempts can
be made to reproduce the sounds of the Hardanger fiddle
in the accompaniments to certain Norwegian songs and
the bania in those to Negro songs.

It is clear that songs intended for this type of treatment
need to be selected with care and they may need to be
transposed if only diatonic instruments are available:
pentatonic songs may be performed in keys of C, F and
G major (or their relative minor). The children themselves should be encouraged to decide which instruments
and style of accompaniment are most suited to the subject
and mood of a song and its national origin.

There is a common tendency in this type of activity to
make use of too many instruments. The teacher, anxious
to ensure that as many children as possible have opportunities to gain instrumental experience, may be tempted
to spend available funds on a large number of inexpensive
instruments and to supplement these by a proliferation
of 'home-made' instruments. A much wiser policy would
be to invest in fewer instruments of good tone quality
and reliable intonation. Percussion instruments should
never be used simply as noisy time-keepers and if not
more than seven children in a class of thirty-five are given
instruments to play there will be less likelihood of the

accompaniment being congested and over-loaded. The more subtle effects which can be achieved with percussion instruments should be explored, as should contrasts in timbre and dynamics. Thus attention should be drawn to the effectiveness of varying the type of accompaniment from verse to verse, according to the words of the song, of introducing occasional instrumental and vocal solos, of reserving tuttis for choruses, climaxes and endings and of including introductions, interludes and postludes, perhaps based upon rhythmic or melodic question-and-answer procedures. Habits of listening attentively to one's own contribution in relation to the total sound are as important in this type of activity as in unison and part-singing and they contribute significantly to the development of general listening skills. Attention should also be given to developing an awareness of the importance of instrumental styles and techniques. For instance, an agile figure devised for playing on the xylophone is unlikely to be suitable for playing on chime bars, the glockenspiel or metallophone. Similarly in the playing of tuned percussion instruments, it is necessary to emphasize the importance of posture, loose wrists, and the positioning of instruments and to encourage playing with alternate hands, the beater being held near the end so that, with a light rebounding action, the sound can be drawn out of the bar.

Rhythmic accompaniments can be provided by the different types of hand clapping referred to in a previous chapter or by percussion instruments. The most elementary form of this type of accompaniment involves the playing of pulse and half-pulse notes and the first beat of the bar in triple time and the first and third beats in quadruple time. Two pairs of claves can be used for this purpose, the lower-pitched pair being played on the strong beats. Rhythmic figures, derived from speech patterns, can be combined with pulse and half-pulse notes and used for introductions, chorus-accompaniments and ostinati. The possibilities of using oriental-style and double ostinati should be investigated and simple syncopated ostinati can be introduced into the accompaniments to such songs as the calypso, 'Mary Ann', and the Mexican folk song, 'Cielito Lindo'. There is a wide range of percussion instruments from which to select: drums (snare, bongo, hand and bass), tambours, triangles, cymbals (including finger, antique and suspended), gongs, Chinese tom-toms, two-tone temple or wood blocks, castanets, tambourines and claves or rhythm sticks, played with one hand cupped as a resonator. Instruments which are shaken include maracas, bells (sleigh, jingle, Indian, wrist and bell-tree) and rattles (box, cane, gourd and jingle). Sand blocks, like the guiro (rasp or resi-resi), are scraped.

Melodic instruments can be used to double the vocal line or, by omitting repeated and passing notes, to play a simplified, outline version of it. A simple descant or counter-melody, involving perhaps a restricted number of notes, can be played by some of the less able children. Melodic ostinati, mainly using the notes 'soh' and 'lah', are often suitable for accompanying pentatonic songs; ostinati can also be easily devised for accompanying rounds. Rhythmic and melodic instruments can be used to create simple sound effects in the accompaniments. 'Hickory, Dickory, Dock' may be taken as a very simple example, two-tone wooden blocks being used for the ticking, xylophone glissandi for 'up' and 'down' and a gong or cymbal for 'struck one'. Wind instruments suitable for class use include recorders, bamboo pipes, melodicas, clarinas and harmonicas. Percussion instruments of definite pitch fall into four groups. Those having wooden bars are xylophones and marimbas, and metal instruments include glockenspiels (sometimes referred to as dulcimers or celestas), chime bars, metallophones, tubular bells and hand-bells; soprano and alto glockenspiels and soprano, alto-soprano, alto and bass xylophones and metallophones are available. Glass instruments are represented by tumblers and wine glasses and stringed instruments by psalteries and Nordic lyres.

Mention was made in the previous chapter of adopting trial-and-error procedures when devising harmonic accompaniments to songs. Drones can form an accompaniment to pentatonic melodies, but at least two chords will be necessary when the complete diatonic scale is involved. Initial harmonic experimentation may be restricted to rounds and simple folk songs which admit of I and V harmonies, if in a major or minor key, or I and VII if modal. Some of the tuned percussion instruments referred to in the previous paragraph can provide harmonic support. These may be used to play the roots of chords and, at a later stage, complete chords may be played by individual children or shared by a group of children. It is possible to play chords on the harmonica, melodica, chordal dulcimer and zither. The autoharp is a useful instrument for harmonic experimentation and establishing tempo and tonality, although its tuning can be a time-consuming process; two children can be involved in playing the autoharp, one depressing the bars and the other stroking the strings. Two children can also share the playing of simple chordal sequences on the piano: regard should be paid to the chordal lay-out in order to avoid confusing changes of hand positions. The open strings of violins, violas and cellos can be played pizzicato or adjacent pairs of strings can be bowed; roots of chords can also be played on the guitar. The bass xylophone, junior timpani and tunable tambours can add an attractive sonority to the texture and prevent its being thin and top-heavy.[9]

MOVEMENT SKILLS

Movement skills will now be briefly discussed.

Several references have been made in the course of this book to the close association between music and movement, the importance of motor imagery in listening, the role of movement in developing rhythmic, formal and stylistic concepts and its value in providing creative outlets for emotional tension, artistic self-expression and aesthetic response. The opportunities which music and movement provides for active participation, on an individual as well as a group basis, can be of particular value to the a-rhythmic child. Movement can also be associated naturally with various musical skills and have a stimulating effect on other expressive work. Mention has also been made of the need for sensitive guidance which, without reducing spontaneity or encouraging stereotyped responses, will enable children to acquire a vocabulary of fundamental locomotor and axial movements. Although such factors as freedom, relaxation, body awareness and motor control must receive attention, it must always be remembered that heightened musical responsiveness is the principal objective: choice of music and quality of performance are therefore matters of considerable importance. Physical response to the structure or to the mood and general expressive qualities of the music may lead to the exploration of free and formalized national and period dances. The scope of music and movement may be extended to include mime[10] and dramatizations of poems by Stevenson, de la Mare and Lear, stories, folk songs and programmatic works as well as of the cantata-like works composed by the children themselves.

LISTENING SKILLS

Finally, *listening skills* will be considered.

'Appreciation' is an unsatisfactory term to describe the skills associated with the receptive series of links in the chain of musical communication. It is a vague term, in that it can refer to enjoyment, understanding or discrimination or any combination of the three elements, it has come to imply pupil-passivity and, most important of all, it is not a separate branch of the curriculum but the most vital of the elements which should be present in every musical activity in which the pupils engage. This last objection can be directed also at the term 'listening', since such activities as singing, playing and movement must obviously be concerned with developing perceptive listening habits. In this sense, the frequently-made assertion that it is better to perform than to listen has unfortunate, if unintentional, implications.

Although active pupil involvement is obviously highly desirable, the commonly-held assumption that the art of listening can be acquired simply through performance is open to serious criticism. Music is essentially an aural art, existing only in time; listening, being an active perceptual experience, is an art which demands sustained and concentrated attention and has to be acquired in the same way as creative and executive skills. The insufficient attention given in the past to the development and guidance of listening habits applies not only to music: in English teaching also, listening comprehension has been neglected and, until the recent investigations into the subject of 'auracy', little research was conducted into listening as a communication skill.[11] It is important that musical educationists give attention to evolving special listening or auding techniques intended to promote listening efficiency, especially since listening is likely to remain the principal post-school musical pastime for the majority of people and since it is possible that music can contribute to the promotion of general auditory development.

The influence of the mass media is responsible for the current habit of treating music simply as a background to other activities. Music has become an almost inescapable phenomenon and there is an increasing tendency to regard all music as *musique d'ameublement* or as a mere auditory aerosol spray. Its ready availability 'on tap' and the volume and distorted quality of sound of much piped or canned music have resulted in a cheapening of music's influence and the emergence of shallow and superficial 'low-level' listening habits. The development of listening skills must therefore be a primary objective of musical education.

Any course in aural training must take into account the importance of tonal memory and the fact that the span of attention of even the most sophisticated listener is limited, because of the considerable physical and mental demands made by attentive listening. This implies the need for the teacher, not only to give careful consideration to the duration of the musical illustrations selected, but also to direct the pupils' listening and develop their powers of musical observation and concentration by focusing their attention on particular features of the music and by making judicious use of well-planned and purposeful repetition.

The listening points selected should be related to the various concepts discussed in the previous chapter. Thus in dealing with programmatic works, attention should be drawn, not simply to the various descriptive effects, but to the methods by which such effects have been achieved. Certain works will be selected in order to focus attention on textural concepts; they may include such works as chorale preludes from Bach's church cantatas, the finale of Franck's Violin Sonata, the Farandole from Bizet's 'L'Arlésienne' Suite no. 2, the Overture to Vaughan Williams's *The Wasps* and 'Conversations between Beauty and the Beast' from Ravel's *Ma Mère l'Oye*. Textural concepts can be developed also by part-singing and hidden melody exercises. There is a plentiful supply of audio-visual material relating to the instruments of the orchestra; concepts of timbre can also be developed by studying the different brass styles associated with military, brass, jazz and dance bands and the less familiar instrumental colours of baroque, oriental and electronic music, by listening to the same work in more than one version (for example for orchestra and military band, piano and harpsichord or harp, cello and guitar) and by considering to which orchestral instruments themes played on the piano would be most appropriately allocated.

Familiarity with principal themes is an important means of achieving attentive listening; works based upon melodies already known to the pupils are thus of obvious value in developing listening skills. Such melodies include nursery songs (Quilter's *Children's Overture*), English folk songs (Vaughan Williams's *English Folk Song Suite* and *Fantasia on Greensleeves* and Holst's *St Paul's suite*) and American traditional songs (Copland's *Appalachian Spring, Billy the Kid*, and *Old American Songs*); 'Frère Jacques' is quoted in the third movement of Mahler's

First Symphony, and 'From Greenland's icy mountains' in Ives's First String Quartet and Fourth Symphony. Principal themes can be sung, tapped, played and, in certain cases, provided by the class with a simple instrumental accompaniment. The notation of such themes can be presented as an aid to concentration and a first step to score reading, and an anthology of themes can be built up in pupils' manuscript books; simple themes can also be used for dictation purposes. A study of chaconnes and dance movements which make prominent use of particular rhythmic patterns can be effectively linked with the use of ostinati in group improvisatory work.

The reading of melodies prepares the ground for score following and eventually score reading. A musical score is a valuable aid to memory, concentration and self-discovery, and it enables the teacher to focus attention on the rhythmic, melodic, formal and instrumental features of the music. To begin with, pupils can follow the scores of chamber works as well as individual orchestral parts; the following of inner parts can develop listening in depth and thus be a useful form of aural training. Older pupils, who are perhaps intending to take music in the G.C.E. examination, may collaborate to play simple orchestral scores on two pianos. It may be argued that, because of the technical problems arising from the use of a number of transposing instruments and clefs, special scores intended for listeners should be published, in addition to the conventional scores intended for performers' use. Simplified and annotated scores are available and various types of graphic notation have been devised. 'Tonescripts', which are available in chart, film-strip and film versions, represent an attempt to make visual effects correspond to aural effects and to reduce the need for verbal analysis and explanation; the instruments are labelled and indicated by the use of colour, the principal thematic material is represented by contours and the sections are numbered. The lay-out of the charts is such that it provides, as it were, an aerial view of the complete work and, if a pointer is used, it can move at a constant speed. The pupils themselves could usefully be given practice in drawing their own simple graphic scores of suitable works.

Repetition has a dual function in music, aesthetic and psychological. Repetition is aesthetically necessary in order to achieve balance, symmetry, unity and cohesion: regular pulsation, imitation, canon and fugue, ostinato, repeated and double expositions, recapitulation, ternary and rondo forms and serial techniques all embody the repetition principle, and sequence, ground bass, theme and variations, development, thematic transformation and concerto cadenzas illustrate the fusion of the twin principles of contrast and repetition. Repetition can be used to achieve widely-differing effects. Thus Wagner's expressive use of it may be compared with Tchaikowsky's and one may contrast Beethovenian repetition with the primitive, hypnotic effects achieved by Stravinsky's use of repeated motives, harmonic pedals and single and multiple ostinati. In so intangible an art form as music, repetition is also a psychological necessity. Although, as has been indicated above, repetition is a built-in feature of musical forms and devices, it would be unreasonable to expect a piece of music to be assimilated at a first hearing: as was pointed out in Chapter 3, controlled, purposeful repetition is necessary if understanding and liking are to develop. Carefully spaced repetitions should be arranged. New listening points should be suggested each time, though occasionally the listening should be of a purely recreational nature. In addition, perhaps one or more lessons could be set aside towards the end of each term for a selection of items to be repeated and placed in their historical context. Members of the class should be encouraged to select some of the pieces and to discuss the reasons for their choice. This can provide a useful guide to the teacher and help to develop the pupils' discriminative ability. Music in morning assembly also provides an excellent opportunity for the repetition of listening experiences.

Several audio-visual aids can be used in the development of listening skills. They include film strips, opaque projectors, used for the projection of non-transparent materials, and overhead projectors; loop films and sound films are particularly valuable when motion is essential to the concept being dealt with and when close-up shots, in slow motion, are required to demonstrate instrumental techniques. Sound and televised broadcasts to schools, which are now placing an increasing emphasis on listener/viewer participation, can make an important contribution to the development of listening skills. A tape recorder can serve a variety of purposes, depending on the quality of its reproduction. In the development of vocal and instrumental skills it can be used to record rehearsals and concerts, accompaniments and one of the parts of a part-song. It can enable a class to listen critically to its own singing and a recorded repertoire of good class singing can be a valuable teaching aid. Because of the problems of precise location and the consequent risk of damaging gramophone records, carefully selected illustrations can be taped for purposes of analysis and repetition; due regard must of course be paid to the laws of copyright. Other subjects which can benefit from the use of a tape recorder include creative work, electronic experimentation with sound patterns, programmed courses of aural training, environmental sounds, acoustics (the tape recorder being used perhaps in conjunction with an oscilloscope), sound effects and incidental music for movement and mime, film strip commentaries and sound broadcasts. The quality of recording and play-back is vitally important: a ribbon or moving coil microphone is preferable to a crystal one and a good external speaker is a wise investment.

Excessive reliance should not, however, be placed upon the mechanical reproduction of music. With the growth of the mass media of communication and the decline in domestic music making, it is not only children from culturally impoverished backgrounds who rarely have the opportunity to hear live performances of serious music. Sustained interest and attentive listening are more likely to be achieved by means of a live performance than a recording: visual interest and appreciation of motor skills influence the listener's response and extend his span of attention. The remarkable degree of communication achieved in the field of 'pop' music is due in part to the interest of members of the audience in the performers as personalities with whom they can identify themselves; listening to anonymous, disembodied sounds from loudspeakers is, by comparison, an unstimulating experience. It follows that the teacher who is able to make effective use in the classroom of his practical skills as a musician is at a considerable advantage. School concerts, visits by small professional ensembles and visits to orchestral concerts and operas can provide a valuable sense of occasion. Special concerts for schools are by no means a recent innovation. Henschel's concerts date from the 1890s, Gwynne Kimpton's from 1911 and Walter Carroll's and Robert Mayer's (modelled on those of Damrosch) from 1923. Recognizing the need to make

more adequate provision for young people in the 14 to
25 age group, Mayer launched 'Youth and Music' in
1954; this was the British equivalent of Marcel Cuvelier's
'Jeunesses Musicales' and it has provided subsidized
performances of operas and orchestral and chamber
music.

INTEGRATION

The fact that the various musical skills have been considered separately does not imply that they should be
practised and developed independently of one another.
The common procedure of allocating one of two weekly
lessons to 'singing' and the other to 'appreciation' may
be administratively convenient, but such a dichotomy is
educationally unsatisfactory since it imposes unnecessary
rigidities on the learning process and ignores the inter-
related nature of musical skills. The practice of fragmen-
tation and tight compartmentalization is gradually being
abandoned. In advanced studies too such arbitrary distinctions as those between harmony and counterpoint and
history and form are ceasing to be recognized. In schools
the attempts to relate musical experiences and achieve an
integrated musical curriculum have taken various forms.
One method has been to make use of centres of interest
which bring together a number of musical skills. Some
of the possible linking themes were referred to in the
discussion of programme music.

A form of musical project that is becoming increasingly
popular involves the composition and performance of
stories with songs and background music, cantatas and
operettas. Such projects enable the teacher, not only to
bring together the various musical skills, but also to
exploit fruitfully the valid inter-relationships existing

between music and other cognate subjects. Although an excessive concern with correlation can result in diffuseness and dilution, such varied activities as verse and prose writing, choral speech, painting, acting, mime and dance can form an integral part of a coherent artistic enterprise. Music in schools has for too long been isolated from those art forms with which, in the time of the Ancient Greeks, it was so naturally associated. Carl Orff, influenced no doubt by the Wagnerian ideal of the community of the arts, his enthusiasm for eurhythmics and his theatrical experience, has persuasively advocated the use of music as a centre of correlation. Music viewed in this broader context, far from being a non-essential embellishment, can be a truly vital educational force.

NOTES TO CHAPTER 5

1 Ehrenzweig, A., *The Psycho-analysis of Artistic Vision and Hearing*, Routledge & Kegan Paul, 1953.
2 Coleman, S. N., *A Children's Symphony*, New York: Bureau of Publications, Teachers College, Columbia University, 1931.
3 Roberts, R., *Musical Instruments made to be played*, Dryad Press, 1965.
4 Boarder, S., *They Made an Opera*, University of London Press, 1966.
5 Plowden Report, *Children and their Primary Schools*, H.M.S.O., 1967.
6 Schools Council, *The Certificate of Secondary Education: Experimental Examinations: Music*, H.M.S.O., 1966.
7 Hadow Report, *The Education of the Adolescent*, H.M.S.O., 1926.
8 Brocklehurst, J. B., *Music in Schools*, Routledge & Kegan Paul, 1962.
9 Winters, G., *Musical Instruments in the Classroom*, Long-

mans, 1967; *An Introduction to Group Music Making*, Chappell, 1967.

10 Gray, V., and Percival, R., *Music, Movement and Mime for Children*, Oxford University Press, 1962.

11 Wilkinson, A. M., and Atkinson, D., 'A Test of Listening Comprehension', *Educational Review*, xviii (1966), No. 3.

INDEX OF NAMES

INDEX OF SUBJECTS

INDEX OF SUBJECTS